Basic
Patterns
in Union
Contracts

Thirteenth Edition

Basic
Patterns
in Union
Contracts

Thirteenth Edition

By the Editors of
Collective Bargaining Negotiations & Contracts

The Bureau of National Affairs, Inc., Washington, D.C.

Published by BNA Books
1250 23rd St., NW, Washington, D.C. 20037-1165

Printed in the United States of America
International Standard Serial Number: 0521-8071
International Standard Book Number: 0-87179-755-0

® GCIU 302-L

Contents

4 ———

Pensions   **27**

5 ———

Grievances and Arbitration   **33**

6 ———

Income Maintenance   **41**

16 ———————————————————————————————

Wages 115

17 ———————————————————————————————

Working Conditions: Safety and Health; Discrimination ... 127

Index **133**

Introduction

This survey outlines the major types of provisions and their frequency in collective bargaining contracts. The purpose of the study is to provide negotiators with comparisons to their own agreements, bargaining proposals, and counterproposals. It further provides data on the most frequent means employed in handling bargaining issues and alternatives commonly used.

A file of about 4,000 agreements is maintained by The Bureau of National Affairs, Inc. These contracts are kept up to date with their latest renewals or amendments. From this file, a sample of 400 contracts is maintained with regard to a cross section of industries, unions, number of employees covered, and geographical areas.

The 400-contract sample forms the basis for analysis in this survey. In a majority of the provisions discussed and accompanying tables, the relative frequencies of particular practices are indicated separately for manufacturing and non-manufacturing contracts. In addition, prevalent industry practices are noted.

A list of the states included in each of the geographic areas analyzed follows:

Middle Atlantic: Delaware, District of Columbia, Maryland, New Jersey, New York, and Pennsylvania.

Midwest: Iowa, Kansas, Minnesota, Missouri, Nebraska, North Dakota, and South Dakota.

New England: Connecticut, Maine, Massachusetts, New Hampshire, Rhode Island, and Vermont.

North Central: Illinois, Indiana, Michigan, Ohio, and Wisconsin.

Rocky Mountain: Colorado, Idaho, Montana, and Wyoming.

Southeast: Alabama, Florida, Georgia, Kentucky, Louisiana, Mississippi, North Carolina, Puerto Rico, South Carolina, Tennessee, Virginia, and West Virginia.

Southwest: Arizona, Nevada, New Mexico, Oklahoma, Texas, and Utah.

West Coast: Alaska, California, Hawaii, Oregon, and Washington.

Caution should be exercised in the use of a sample analysis of this type:

(1) All frequency figures apply only to the contract sample studied. To the extent that the sample is broadly representative, these figures approximate general practice.

(2) There is some "turnover" in contracts making up the sample from year to year. Replacement of agreements generally is caused by company dissolution or union decertification. The representative character of the sample is not significantly affected, however, by substitutions.

(3) More than one of the possible practices on any major bargaining issue may appear together in the same contract. Consequently, caution should be used in totalling different columns in the tabular presentation. Also, some percentages given for the frequency of various practices on the same subject do not total 100 percent because some contracts do not refer to the subject at all. In other cases, percentages do not total exactly 100 percent because of rounding to the nearest whole number.

(4) The presence of certain provisions in some contracts and their absence in others may be due to such different factors as varying industry conditions or merely the special emphasis given by company or union negotiators in the industries concerned.

(5) Caution also should be exercised in the comparison of figures in any current study with figures from a previous study. Sampling variations may introduce small percentage changes—either upwards or downwards—which do not reflect actual changes in contract practice. It is advisable, therefore, to avoid placing too great emphasis upon small percentage changes from one study to another. Larger changes more reliably connote changes in actual contract practice.

1

Amendment and Duration

A majority (74 percent) of contracts in the study have three-year terms and 5 percent run for two years. Only three sample contracts are in effect for one year. The percentage of contracts with a duration of four or more years continued a steady climb, rising from 5 percent in 1986 to 9 percent in 1989 and to 21 percent in this analysis.

Geographic analysis of the Basic Patterns database shows three-year agreements predominating in all regions, ranging from 40 percent in the Rocky Mountain area to 83 percent in the Southeast area.

One-year agreements make up only 1 percent of the sample. One contract each with this duration is found in the apparel, maritime, and rubber industries.

Two-year contract terms account for 5 percent of the sample, compared with 9 percent in the 1989 study and 13 percent in 1986. Two-year contracts appear in 3 percent of manufacturing contracts and in 8 percent of non-manufacturing.

Industry pattern: Thirty-nine percent of the 26 industries in the study have at least one contract with a two-year duration. At least 10 percent of contracts in services (22 percent), chemicals (13 percent), and electrical machinery, foods, communications, construction, and textiles (each 10 percent) have two-year durations.

Three-year contracts are found in 76 percent of manufacturing contracts and in 69 percent of non-manufacturing agreements.

Industry pattern: All leather, petroleum, and utilities contracts in the sample have three-year terms. A petroleum industry tradition of negotiating two-year contracts was broken in 1990 bargaining, thus all sample contracts analyzed in this study were to run for three years.

Other industries in which three-year contracts prevail are stone-clay-glass (92 percent), apparel (89 percent), chemicals (88 percent), insurance and finance and foods (each 86 percent), electrical machinery (85 percent), furniture (83 percent), and textiles (80 percent).

Longer term agreements—four years or more—rose from 9 percent in the 1989 study to 20 percent in the manufacturing sector and from 10 percent in 1989 to 23 percent in the non-manufacturing sector.

Industry pattern: Of the 400 contracts, 83 have terms of four years or longer—48 manufacturing contracts and 35 non-manufacturing. Durations of four years or more are found in at least 30 percent of contracts in paper (57 percent), printing (50 percent), maritime (38 percent), fabricated metals (37 percent), primary metals (36 percent), and retail and mining (each 33 percent).

Length of Contract Term

(Frequency Expressed as Percentage of Industry Contracts)

	Duration in Years*			
	1	2	3	4 or more
ALL INDUSTRIES	1	5	74	21
MANUFACTURING	1	3	76	20
Apparel	11	—	89	—
Chemicals	—	13	88	—
Electrical Machinery	—	10	85	5
Fabricated Metals	—	—	63	37
Foods	—	10	86	5
Furniture	—	—	83	17
Leather	—	—	100	—
Lumber	—	—	71	29
Machinery	—	—	77	23
Paper	—	—	43	57
Petroleum	—	—	100	—
Primary Metals	—	—	64	36
Printing	—	—	50	50
Rubber	17	—	67	17
Stone-Clay-Glass	—	—	92	8
Textiles	—	10	80	10
Transportation Equipment	—	3	79	18
NON-MANUFACTURING	1	8	69	23
Communications	—	10	70	20
Construction	—	10	66	24
Insurance & Finance	—	—	86	14
Maritime	13	—	50	38
Mining	—	8	58	33
Retail	—	—	67	33
Services	—	22	67	11
Transportation	—	4	72	24
Utilities	—	—	100	—

*Included in each yearly grouping are some contracts with durations of within six months of the specified year(s).

Contract Reopeners

Reopening of a contract for amendment prior to the scheduled expiration date is called for in 6 percent of the sample, down from 11 percent in the 1989 study and 14 percent in the 1986 analysis. Reopener provisions appear more frequently in non-manufacturing (8 percent) than in manufacturing (5 percent) agreements.

Seventy-six percent of these reopener provisions permit reopening for negotiation of wages, 32 percent for benefits, and 12 percent for cost-of-living adjustments. A contract, in some cases, may be reopened for more than one reason.

Reasons for Contract Reopenings

(Frequency Expressed as Number of Contracts with Reopener Provisions)

Reopening Allowed	All Industries	Manu-facturing	Non-manu-facturing
For Wages	19	11	8
For Benefits	8	3	5
For Cost-of-Living Adjustments	3	2	1

When a contract may be reopened is specified in all but three agreements with reopener provisions. Of these, 27 percent allow for reopening at any time with or without a limit on the number of times per year the contract may be reopened. Seventy-three percent specify a set date or period of time during which a reopener may be permitted.

Impasse in reopener talks is discussed in forty percent of the contracts with reopener provisions. Of impasse provisions, 70 percent permit strikes and/or lockouts, 10 percent provide for cancellation or suspension of the agreement, and another 10 percent call for arbitration. The option to strike and/or lock out appears in 71 percent of impasse clauses in manufacturing and in 67 percent in non-manufacturing.

Industry pattern: Reopener provisions are found in agreements in six of the 17 manufacturing industries and in seven of the nine non-manufacturing industries. Such provisions appear in at least 25 percent of contracts in textiles (50 percent), printing (38 percent), rubber (33 percent), and leather (25 percent).

Contract Renewal

Most agreements provide for extension past their expiration date unless action is taken to amend or terminate. Automatic renewal provisions are found in 85 percent of agreements in the sample. Eighty-six percent of contracts calling for automatic renewal specify annual renewals. One percent specify renewal for three-year periods, and 14 percent specify renewal for indefinite periods. Renewal clauses occur with about the same frequency in manufacturing agreements as in non-manufacturing contracts.

Industry pattern: At least one-half of contracts in all industries provide for automatic renewal, most often with annual extensions. Renewal for an indefinite period is most common in the petroleum industry (86 percent).

Notice that a party desires to terminate or modify the agreement is explicitly stated in 92 percent of sample contracts. This requirement is found with nearly the same frequency in manufacturing (93 percent) as in non-manufacturing (91 percent) agreements. Fourteen percent of notice requirements specify that proposed changes accompany the notice, and 30 percent specify when negotiations must begin.

Clauses requiring notice of a wish to amend or terminate are found in at least 80 percent of contracts in all industries except maritime and printing (each 75 percent), and apparel (67 percent). A requirement that proposed changes accompany such notice appears in 50 percent of leather agreements, and in at least 30 percent of utilities (40 percent), chemicals (38 percent), and mining (33 percent) contracts.

A clause specifying when negotiations must begin appears in all rubber contracts and in at least one-half of all agreements in four industries—petroleum (57 percent), primary metals (56 percent), and leather and mining (each 50 percent).

Renegotiation of Contract

A minority (20 percent) of contracts make explicit provision for the status of the agreement when renewal negotiations extend beyond the expiration date. Such provisions are more common in manufacturing (24 percent) than in non-manufacturing (14 percent) contracts. Of these provisions, 38 percent call for extension only by mutual agreement, 19 percent call for automatic extension for a specified period with further extensions only by mutual agreement, and 44 percent call for automatic extension.

Eighteen percent of contracts included in this survey discuss problems arising from stalemated talks during bargaining. Of these, 55 percent specify that strikes and/or lockouts may be permitted; 38 percent state that the agreement may be terminated either automatically or by one of the parties; 7 percent call for arbitration (either mandatory or by mutual consent).

Amendment and Duration Provisions

(Frequency Expressed as Percentage of Contracts in Each Region*)

	All Regions	Middle Atlantic	Midwest	New England	North Central	Rocky Mountain	Southeast	Southwest	West Coast	Multiregion
Term of Contract**										
One year	1	1	—	—	—	10	—	—	—	2
Two years	5	2	7	8	5	20	4	8	2	6
Three years	74	79	79	69	72	40	83	77	80	58
Four or more years	21	17	14	23	23	30	13	15	18	35
Reopener Provisions	6	2	7	—	4	20	17	8	2	10
Separability Provision	65	59	64	58	60	70	64	77	82	71
Successorship Clause	43	46	46	50	44	10	36	15	44	46

* See p. xi for area designations.

** Included in each yearly grouping are some contracts with durations within six months of the specified year(s).

Separability

The possibility that a portion of a contract may conflict with a state or federal law is considered in 65 percent of the sample. Nearly one-half (47 percent) of these provisions simply state that the offending section shall be declared null and void without affecting other provisions. Forty-three percent of these clauses call for renegotiation of the matter; the remainder (10 percent) state that the illegal section shall be modified to conform with the law.

Separability provisions appear in 74 percent of non-manufacturing contracts, compared to 60 percent of manufacturing agreements. Under agreements containing separability provisions, renegotiation of illegal clauses is more prevalent in non-manufacturing (59 percent) than in manufacturing (30 percent); nullification is more prevalent in manufacturing (58 percent) than in non-manufacturing (33 percent); modification to conform with the law is more prevalent in manufacturing (12 percent) than in non-manufacturing (9 percent).

Industry pattern: Separability provisions are found in all industries and appear in at least one-half of the contracts in 19 of the 26 industries. Among those industries with the highest proportion of such provisions are: apparel, leather, and petroleum (each 100 percent); construction (90 percent); printing (88 percent); retail and services (each 85 percent); rubber (83 percent); and communications (80 percent).

Successorship Clauses

Successorship clauses stipulate that any change in management shall not invalidate the agreement, but rather that the new management must assume the contractual obligations of the predecessor. These clauses appear in 43 percent of agreements included in this study, unchanged from the 1989 study.

Industry pattern: Successorship clauses are more common in non-manufacturing (50 percent) than in manufacturing (38 percent) contracts. At least one-half of the contracts in nine industries contain such provisions: apparel (78 percent), transportation (64 percent), communications and utilities (each 60 percent), insurance and finance (57 percent), retail (56 percent), foods (52 percent), and furniture and rubber (each 50 percent).

2

Discharge, Discipline, and Resignation

Discharge and discipline provisions are found in 98 percent of the 400 contracts analyzed. These clauses are included in all but one manufacturing agreement and excluded in only eight non-manufacturing contracts. Geographic analysis reveals that discharge-discipline provisions are contained in from 90 percent to 100 percent of agreements in all areas designated in the Basic Patterns database.

Grounds For Discharge

Grounds for discharge, found in 97 percent of sample contracts, are of two types—discharge for "cause" or "just cause" or discharge for specific offenses. Many contracts contain both "cause" or "just cause" and specific provisions.

"Cause" or "just cause" is stated as a reason for discharge in 91 percent of agreements studied—94 percent in manufacturing and 86 percent in non-manufacturing.

Industry pattern: Employees may be discharged for "cause" or "just cause" under all communications, electrical machinery, fabricated metals, foods, furniture, leather, machinery, paper, and petroleum agreements and in at least 70 percent of contracts in all other industries except maritime and printing.

Specific grounds for discharge are found in 84 percent of contracts in the database (91 percent in manufacturing and 73 percent in non-manufacturing). Grounds most frequently referred to in sample agreements are: violation of leave provisions, 55 percent; unauthorized absence, 50 percent; participation in unauthorized strikes, 41 percent; dishonesty or theft, 26 percent; intoxication, 23 percent; incompetence or failure to meet standards and violation of company rules, each 20 percent; insubordination and misconduct, each 18 percent; failure to obey safety rules, 13 percent; and tardiness, 9 percent.

Industry pattern: Specific grounds for discharge are found in all lumber, paper, printing, rubber, and textiles agreements and in at least 63 percent of contracts in all other industries except communications (50 percent) construction (41 percent) and petroleum (14 percent).

Violation of leave is mentioned as a reason for dismissal in 65 percent of manufacturing agreements and 39 percent of those in non-manufacturing. This cause for discharge appears under all rubber agreements and in 84 percent of primary metals, 83 percent of furniture, 79 percent of fabricated metals, 77 percent of machinery, 75 percent each of chemicals, electrical machinery, and leather, 74 percent of retail, 71 percent of transportation equipment, 57 percent each of foods, insurance and finance, and paper, and in 50 percent each of mining and textiles agreements.

Unauthorized absence is cause for discharge in 63 percent of manufacturing agreements and in 28 percent of non-manufacturing contracts. Dismissals due to unauthorized absences are most common in machinery (88 percent), furniture and rubber (each 83 percent), transportation equipment (82 percent), fabricated metals (79 percent), electrical machinery (75 percent), primary metals (72 percent), lumber (71 percent), stone-clay-glass (62 percent), paper (57 percent), and leather and textiles agreements (each 50 percent).

Unauthorized strike participation is cause for discharge in 48 percent of manufacturing and in 30 percent of non-manufacturing agreements. Such provisions are found in 90 percent of textiles contracts, 67 percent of apparel, 59 percent of transportation equipment, 55 percent of electrical machinery, 54 percent of stone-clay-glass, 52 percent of primary metals, and in 50 percent each of furniture, leather, maritime, mining, paper, and utilities agreements.

Dishonesty or theft is listed as a reason for discharge in 21 percent of manufacturing and 33 percent of non-manufacturing agreements. This cause for discharge appears most frequently in paper (71 percent), retail (63 percent), services (52 percent), and transportation (40 percent).

Intoxication may lead to discharge in 18 percent of manufacturing agreements and 30 percent of non-manufacturing agreements. Intoxication most frequently is specified as a reason for discharge in the following industries: paper (71 percent), retail (52 percent), maritime (50 percent), and services (48 percent).

Incompetence or failure to meet standards is cause for dismissal in 20 percent of manufacturing and 18 percent of non-manufacturing contracts. This reason for discharge is found in 50 percent of paper, 38 percent each of maritime and printing, and in at least 30 percent of contracts in electrical machinery, retail, services, and stone-clay-glass.

Violation of company rules is cause for dismissal in 23 percent of manufacturing agreements and in 14 percent of non-manufacturing contracts. It is specified in 57 percent each of lumber and paper contracts, 38 percent of printing, and in at least 30 percent of furniture (33 percent) and textiles (30 percent).

Insubordination is a reason for dismissal in 19 percent of manufacturing contracts and 16 percent of non-manufacturing contracts. Discharge for insubordination is specified in 64 percent of paper, 33 percent each of furniture, retail, and services, 32 percent of fabricated metals, and 30 percent of textiles agreements.

Misconduct is stated as cause for discharge in 18 percent each of manufacturing and non-manufacturing agreements. It is cause for dismissal in 50 percent each of furniture, maritime, and paper, 43 percent of insurance and finance, 30 percent each of electrical machinery and services, 29 percent of lumber, 26 percent of fabricated metals, 25 percent each of leather and mining, and 20 percent of textiles contracts.

Failure to obey safety rules is cause for discharge in 14 percent of manufacturing and 11 percent of non-manufacturing contracts. This reason for discharge appears in 50 percent of paper, 38 percent of maritime, 33 percent of furniture, and 25 percent each of leather and mining agreements.

Tardiness is cause for discharge in 13 percent of manufacturing and 3 percent of non-manufacturing agreements. It is most often specified in agreements in leather (50 percent), furniture (33 percent), lumber (29 percent), and electrical machinery (25 percent).

Often, causes for discharge listed above are sufficient grounds for immediate discharge. Many contracts, however, allow a number of offenses before an employee is terminated.

Discharge Procedures

Procedures for discharge are found in 67 percent of contracts in the database. These clauses appear in 71 percent of manufacturing and 59 percent of non-manufacturing agreements. Provisions vary considerably and may require that the union be notified in advance of discharge or be present during discharge, that a predischarge hearing be held, or that a written notice be given to the employee, the union, or both.

Discharge Procedures

(Frequency Expressed as Percentage of Contracts)

	Notice			
	To Union (Before or During Discharge)	To Union (After Discharge)	To Employee or Union or Both in Writing	Hearings Before Discharge
All Industries	29	28	41	20
Manufacturing	36	26	40	26
Non-manufacturing	19	32	43	11

Predischarge hearings are called for under 20 percent of contracts surveyed (26 percent of manufacturing and 11 percent of non-manufacturing agreements). Under these provisions, an employee usually is suspended for a given number of days during which a hearing is to take place. Of agreements allowing predischarge hearings, 98 percent state that a union representative may be present.

Industry pattern: Predischarge hearings are most common in fabricated metals (58 percent), mining (50 percent), primary metals (48 percent), and machinery and transportation equipment (each 38 percent).

Advance notice of discharge is given to the union or a union representative is present during the discharge proceedings under 29 percent of agreements—36 percent in manufacturing and 19 percent in non-manufacturing. Twenty-eight percent of contracts (26 percent of manufacturing and 32 percent of non-manufacturing) require that notice be given to the union after discharge.

Industry pattern: Notice to the union (either before, during, or after discharge) is required most frequently in leather (100 percent), mining and rubber (each 83 percent), primary metals (76 percent), insurance and finance and transportation equipment (each 71 percent), and is included in at least 60 percent of contracts in communications, electrical machinery, fabricated metals, foods, machinery, services, textiles, and transportation.

Written notice of discharge is given to the employee, union, or both under 41 percent of agreements—40 percent of manufacturing and 43 percent of non-manufacturing contracts.

Industry pattern: This requirement most often appears in leather (75 percent), insurance and finance (71 percent), services (70 percent), rubber (67 percent), printing (63 percent), transportation (60 percent), fabricated metals (53 percent), and mining (50 percent) agreements.

Discharge Provisions

(Frequency Expressed as Percentage of Contracts in Each Region*)

	Discharge for Cause	Specific Grounds for Discharge	Notice to Union of Discharge	Written Explanation of Discharge	Appeals from Discharge
All Regions	91	84	58	41	88
Middle Atlantic	89	81	62	35	84
Midwest	100	86	54	36	79
New England	92	77	42	31	89
North Central	93	91	65	46	91
Rocky Mountain	80	80	30	30	70
Southeast	92	98	53	38	92
Southwest	92	77	39	31	92
West Coast	89	82	49	38	87
Multiregion	89	69	67	60	94

* See p. xi for area designations.

Appeals Procedures

Discharge may be appealed under 88 percent of contracts studied—91 percent of manufacturing and 83 percent of non-manufacturing agreements.

Industry pattern: Provisions for appeals from discharge appear in all communications, fabricated metals, furniture, insurance and finance, leather, petroleum, printing, and rubber industry agreements and in at least 63 percent of contracts in all other industries except construction (45 percent).

Special time limits within which discharges must be appealed are imposed in 63 percent of contracts in the database. Under these provisions, the most common limits are 5 days (30 percent), 10 days (20 percent), 3 days (16 percent), 7 days (10 percent), 2 days (6 percent), and 15 days (5 percent).

Appeals Procedures

(Frequency Expressed as Number of Contracts)

	Time Limit in Days				Reinstatement	
	1-5	6-10	11-20	Over 20	Full Back Pay	Pay At Arbiter's Discretion
All Industries	137	78	24	12	84	83
Manufacturing	111	40	9	3	54	60
Non-manufacturing	26	38	15	9	30	23

Reinstatement with Back Pay

Reinstatement with back pay for employees improperly discharged is required in 44 percent of sample contracts—49 percent of manufacturing and 36 percent of non-manufacturing agreements. Of these provisions, 48 percent grant full back pay, 48 percent leave the amount awarded to the arbiter's discretion, and 4 percent place a limitation on the amount awarded. In some instances unemployment compensation or money earned from other jobs may be deducted from back pay.

Industry pattern: Reinstatement with back pay is mentioned in all rubber agreements, in 83 percent of furniture, 75 percent of leather, 70 percent each of textiles and utilities, and in 57 percent each of contracts in insurance and finance, lumber, and petroleum.

Discipline Short of Discharge

Disciplinary measures short of discharge are contained in 70 percent of contracts analyzed. These provisions are found in 76 percent of manufacturing and 61 percent of non-manufacturing contracts.

Seventy-three percent of contracts analyzed mention one or more of the following types of disciplinary measures—suspension, layoff, transfer, and demotion. Of these contracts, 93 percent refer to suspension, 26 percent to layoff, 9 percent to demotion, and 2 percent to transfer.

Warning before disciplinary action is called for in 45 percent of contracts in the database—47 percent in manufacturing and 41 percent in non-manufacturing. Of these clauses, 42 percent require that the employee be warned before disciplinary action is taken; 58 percent specify that the employee and union be warned.

Industry pattern: Warning provisions are found in 70 percent of textiles, 67 percent each of rubber and services, 64 percent of primary metals, 63 percent of retail, and 60 percent of electrical machinery agreements. Such clauses also appear in at least one-half of contracts in mining (58 percent), paper (57 percent), foods (52 percent), and leather, machinery, and transportation equipment (each 50 percent).

Notice to the union before, during, or after disciplinary action is required in 51 percent of sample contracts—58 percent in manufacturing and 41 percent in non-manufacturing. Of these, 54 percent require that the union either be notified in advance of discipline or be present during the disciplinary proceedings. The remainder require notice to the union after the fact.

Industry pattern: Notice to the union of disciplinary action is required by all rubber contracts, 83 percent of those in mining, 80 percent of primary metals, 75 percent in electrical machinery and leather, 70 percent in textiles, 68 percent in transportation equipment, 67 percent in furniture, 63 percent in services, and 62 percent in foods.

"Statute of limitations" clauses, under which past offenses are removed from an employee's record after a specified period of time, appear in 40 percent of contracts analyzed. Limitations appear in 45 percent of manufacturing and 32 percent of non-manufacturing contracts.

Industry pattern: These clauses appear in 83 percent of rubber agreements, 75 percent of those in leather, 68 percent of primary metals, 67 percent each of mining and services, 57 percent of paper, and 50 percent each of textiles and transportation equipment agreements.

Resignation Procedures

Resignation procedures are found in only 10 percent of contracts in the database—6 percent in manufacturing and 15 percent in non-manufacturing agreements. All but three of the resignation procedures provisions require prior notification to the employer, and 53 percent impose a penalty for failure to give advance notice.

3

Insurance

Insurance benefits are mentioned in most of the 400 contracts in CBNC's Basic Patterns database. Some contracts include fully detailed plans, others contain only statements or amendments referring to existing benefits, and still others merely stipulate the employer's contribution to an existing health and welfare plan.

The following analysis is based on 225 plans for which sufficient detail on insurance benefits was available.

A rise over the last three years in the percentage of comprehensive medical care plans that replace basic hospitalization and surgical benefits and cover major medical expenses has caused a corresponding decline in the percentage of traditional plans providing these benefits. Forty-eight percent of plans in this year's survey provide comprehensive medical coverage, up from 37 percent in the 1989 study. Basic hospitalization benefits are provided in 52 percent of sample plans (down from 63 percent in the 1989 survey), surgical in 52 percent (down from 61 percent), and major medical in 46 percent (down from 57 percent).

The percentage of plans providing life insurance (99 percent) was unchanged from the 1989 analysis, while the percentage of plans providing coverage for prescription drugs increased to 47 percent from 41 percent. Since the 1989 study, there has been a slight decrease in the number of plans providing coverage for sickness and accident, accidental death and dismemberment, dental, and vision care benefits.

Employee Insurance Coverage

(Frequency Expressed as Percentage of Plans)

	Life	AD&D	S&A	Hosp.	Surg.	Maj. Med.	Comp. Med.	Dent.
All Industries	99	72	81	52	52	46	48	82
Manufacturing	99	76	90	54	54	47	47	77
Non-manufacturing	97	65	62	49	49	44	52	93

Life Insurance

Provision for life insurance is included in 99 percent of the analyzed plans. Maximum coverage of $10,000 or more is called for in 83 percent of the plans specifying amounts of life insurance benefits, up from 81 percent in the 1989 study, 74 percent in 1986, and 63 percent in 1983. Fourteen percent of these clauses provide coverage ranging from $5,000 to $9,000, and 3 percent offer coverage of less than $5,000.

Under plans specifying benefit amounts, 88 percent of those in manufacturing and 70 percent of those in non-manufacturing provide maximum coverage of $10,000 or more. Employees may purchase additional coverage at their own expense under 29 percent of manufacturing plans and 27 percent of non-manufacturing plans providing for life insurance.

Of programs indicating a formula for determining employees' life insurance benefits, 74 percent provide a flat amount for all employees, 24 percent scale benefits to employees' earnings, and 3 percent scale benefits to length of service.

Service requirements for coverage are included in 64 percent of life insurance provisions. Of the service requirement clauses, 25 percent specify one month, 17 percent specify two months, 37 percent specify three months, and 15 percent specify six months.

Almost one-half (47 percent) of the analyzed life insurance provisions allow employees to change from group to individual coverage upon separation, 15 percent specify that employees may convert insurance upon retirement, and 5 percent permit conversion upon layoff.

Post-retirement group life insurance coverage, usually paid by the company, is provided in 51 percent of the plans—57 percent in manufacturing and 36 percent in non-manufacturing. Of plans providing post-retirement group coverage, 71 percent state that the amount of coverage declines immediately upon retirement, and 25 percent state that the amount declines gradually.

Company-paid group coverage during layoffs is included in 53 percent of manufacturing and 27 percent of non-manufacturing plans providing life insurance benefits. Of plans specifying length of coverage during layoffs, 18 percent extend coverage for one month, 18 percent for three months, 12 percent for six months, 19 percent for one year, and 15 percent for two years; 2 percent state that coverage will last for the duration of the layoff.

Transition and bridge benefits are called for in 11 percent of the sample plans—all in manufacturing. More than three-fourths (84 percent) of transition provisions specify a set monthly benefit for two years to survivors of covered employees. Bridge benefits usually follow transition benefits and are payable monthly until the survivor either remarries or becomes eligible for social security. Coverage ranges from $100 to $600 per month, with $400 prevailing.

The cost of employees' life insurance coverage is paid by the company under 87 percent of life insurance plans discussing costs, while under 12 percent the cost is shared by the company and the employee. Only 25 percent of surveyed life insurance plans provide coverage for dependents; in almost all cases (96 percent) the amount of coverage is less than employee coverage. Of plans referring to costs for dependents, coverage is paid by the employer under 28 percent; the employer and employee share costs under 14 percent; and the employee alone pays the costs under 59 percent.

Industry pattern: Life insurance coverage is provided in every analyzed plan in manufacturing except for one in transportation equipment and in every plan in non-manufacturing except for one plan each in retail and utilities.

Employee Insurance Benefits

(Frequency Expressed as Percentage of Plans)

	Life Insurance	A D & D	Sickness and Accident	Hospitalization	Surgical	Major Medical	Doctor's Visits	Misc. Medical Expenses	Comprehensive Medical	Dental	Optical
ALL INDUSTRIES	99	72	81	52	52	46	29	44	48	82	43
MANUFACTURING	99	76	90	54	54	47	32	47	47	77	39
Apparel	100	—	100	100	100	33	100	100	—	—	67
Chemicals	100	70	100	20	20	20	10	20	80	100	20
Electrical Machinery	100	75	92	58	58	58	33	50	42	75	42
Fabricated Metals	100	58	100	50	50	33	50	42	50	58	33
Foods	100	60	80	70	70	60	50	70	30	100	80
Furniture	100	100	100	50	50	50	50	50	50	50	50
Leather	100	100	100	—	—	—	—	—	100	—	—
Lumber	100	33	100	67	67	67	17	5J	33	33	17
Machinery	100	80	95	60	60	60	35	45	40	85	35
Paper	100	100	100	13	13	13	13	13	88	75	25
Petroleum	100	25	50	25	25	25	—	25	75	100	—
Primary Metals	100	89	100	72	72	72	44	67	28	83	56
Printing	100	75	50	25	25	25	—	—	75	100	25
Rubber	100	100	100	83	83	83	83	67	17	67	33
Stone, Clay & Glass	100	86	86	86	86	86	29	71	14	86	43
Textiles	100	100	100	29	29	29	14	29	71	86	—
Transportation Equipment	96	80	72	52	52	28	20	48	48	80	52
NON-MANUFACTURING	97	65	62	49	49	44	24	40	52	93	52
Communications	100	33	50	17	17	17	—	17	83	100	50
Construction	100	100	57	29	29	29	29	57	71	71	57
Insurance & Finance	100	67	67	33	33	33	—	—	67	100	33
Maritime	100	100	100	67	67	67	—	—	33	100	67
Mining	100	67	100	50	50	50	17	33	50	100	33
Retail	92	92	92	62	62	62	39	54	39	92	69
Services	100	62	46	62	62	46	31	54	39	92	46
Transportation	100	39	46	54	54	46	23	39	46	100	46
Utilities	75	25	—	25	25	25	25	25	75	75	50

Accidental Death and Dismemberment Insurance _____

Coverage for accidental death and dismemberment is provided in 72 percent of the surveyed plans, including 76 percent in manufacturing and 65 percent in non-manufacturing.

Of plans specifying the amount payable in the event of death, 69 percent provide the beneficiary an amount equal to the life insurance benefit, and 14 percent provide an amount equal to one-half or less of life insurance. Dismemberment payments generally are equal to one-half the life insurance benefit for loss of either a foot, hand, or eye, and the full amount for loss of any two. Under accidental death and dismemberment plans that mention costs, 86 percent state that the cost of the insurance will be paid by the employer.

Industry pattern: Accidental death and dismemberment benefits are included in all surveyed plans in construction, furniture, leather, maritime, paper, rubber, and textiles; and in at least one-half of all other industries except apparel, communications, lumber, petroleum, transportation, and utilities.

Sickness and Accident Insurance

Provision for non-occupational sickness and accident benefits is found in 81 percent of the analyzed plans—90 percent in manufacturing and 62 percent in non-manufacturing.

Of plans that include a formula for sickness and accident benefits, 52 percent call for a flat amount per week. While weekly payments range from $40 to $325, the two most common payments are $150 and $180. Under 27 percent of the benefit formulas, the weekly amount varies according to the pay scale, and under 21 percent, the amount is a fixed percentage of an employee's weekly pay.

Benefits extend for 26 weeks under 37 percent of plans providing S&A insurance and for 52 weeks under 22 percent. Seventy-six percent of the plans require a waiting period; sickness benefits most often begin on the eighth day, while accident benefits most often begin on the first day.

Of sickness and accident plans referring to costs, 88 percent specify that coverage will be paid solely by the employer.

Industry pattern: Non-occupational sickness and accident benefits are provided in all available plans in apparel, chemicals, fabricated metals, furniture, leather, lumber, maritime, mining, paper, primary metals, rubber, and textiles. They appear in at least one-half of available plans in all other industries except services, transportation, and utilities.

S&A benefits extend for 13 weeks in most available plans in construction and leather; for 26 weeks in most plans in apparel, lumber, paper, and transportation; and for 52 weeks in most plans in rubber and transportation equipment.

Occupational Accident Insurance

Benefits supplementing workers' compensation are included in 26 percent of available plans. Under 63 percent of these provisions, the amount payable is the difference between workers' compensation and the non-occupational sickness and accident rate. All but two plans specifying who will pay for occupational accident insurance state that the employer will pay the full cost.

Long-Term Disability Insurance

Benefits that become payable at the expiration of sickness and accident benefits or after a specified period of time are included in 21 percent of the surveyed plans. While the duration of benefits varies considerably, 30 percent of plans dealing with the subject specify payment of benefits until retirement or for the duration of the disability. The cost of insurance most often is paid by the employer.

Hospitalization Insurance

Coverage for hospitalization expenses is provided in 52 percent of analyzed plans—54 percent in manufacturing plans and 49 percent in non-manufacturing. Of plans providing hospitalization benefits, 21 percent provide coverage through a service plan such as Blue Cross, while 13 percent state that the plan will be underwritten by a commercial carrier.

More than one-third (38 percent) of the hospitalization provisions permit employees to choose between different types of coverage. In most of these cases, coverage by a health maintenance organization (HMO) or preferred provider organization (PPO) is offered as an alternative to traditional fee-for-service coverage.

Under 82 percent of hospitalization plans detailing coverage, benefits include the total daily room and board charge for a semi-private room. Two percent of the hospitalization coverage provisions base coverage on the semi-private room rate but set a maximum amount of coverage per day. Five percent of these clauses set a flat rate per day, with a median of $150.

Duration of hospital benefits is specified in 92 percent of plans outlining hospital insurance coverage. Of these, 37 percent provide coverage for one year, 18 percent for two years, 17 percent for 120 days, and 13 percent for 70 days.

Coverage for items other than room and board, such as medication, special treatment, and therapy, is mentioned in 86 percent of hospitalization plans detailing benefits. Of plans specifying coverage for extras, 86 percent set no limit, 11 percent limit coverage to a specified amount, and 3 percent pay a specified percentage of charges.

Hospitalization for dependents of employees is covered in 97 percent of hospitalization plans. Of these, 98 percent provide coverage equal to that of employees.

The cost of an employee's hospitalization insurance is mentioned in all but three of the plans. Of these, 76 percent provide that the employer will pay the full cost and 24 percent state that the employer and employee will share the cost. Of plans specifying who pays for dependent hospitalization coverage, 69 percent provide that the employer will pay the full cost, 2 percent say that the employee will pay the full cost, and 29 percent state that the employer and the employee will share the expense.

Industry pattern: Hospitalization insurance is called for in every analyzed plan in apparel and in at least one-half of all other industries except chemicals, communications, construction, insurance and finance, leather, paper, petroleum, printing, textiles, and utilities, where comprehensive plans prevail.

Surgical Insurance

Surgical insurance is found in 52 percent of the sample plans, including 54 percent in manufacturing and 49 percent in non-manufacturing. Of analyzed plans, 21 percent specify surgical coverage through a service program such as Blue Shield; 13 percent specify coverage by a commercial carrier. Thirty-seven percent of surgical plans grant employees a choice of coverage through a service or commercial plan or through an HMO or PPO.

The amount of surgical benefits is limited to usual and customary rates in 56 percent of plans specifying amounts and is fixed by schedule in 45 percent. Almost one-third (30 percent) of surgical provisions detailing benefits specify a maximum amount of coverage, ranging from $300 to $25,000.

Surgical insurance for dependents is discussed in 96 percent of surgical plans and in all cases is equal to employees' coverage.

Of plans specifying who pays the cost of employees' surgical insurance, 76 percent state that coverage is paid entirely by the company; the remainder state that the employer and employee share costs. Under plans mentioning costs for dependent coverage, 68 percent state that the employer pays, 29 percent provide that the employer and employee share costs, and 3 percent state that the employee alone pays for dependent surgical insurance.

Industry pattern: Surgical insurance is provided in every available plan in apparel and is included in at least one-half of analyzed plans in every other industry except chemicals, communications, construction, insurance and finance, leather, paper, petroleum, printing, textiles, and utilities, where comprehensive plans prevail.

Major Medical Insurance

Insurance covering costs in excess of basic hospitalization and surgical insurance is found in 46 percent of the analyzed plans—47 percent in manufacturing and 44 percent in non-manufacturing.

Of major medical programs analyzed, 85 percent specify an initial deductible amount before coverage becomes effective. Fifty-six percent of these provisions specify a $100 deductible per person, 14 percent specify $50, and 24 percent specify more than $100. Of plans mentioning family deductibles, 37 percent specify $300 and 23 percent specify $200.

Ninety-seven percent of major medical plans that state the amount of coverage after the deductible contain an 80-20 coinsurance factor, under which the carrier pays 80 percent; two percent contain a 90-10 factor.

Seventeen percent of major medical plans specify annual maximum out-of-pocket expenditures per individual, after which the plan pays all costs. Of these, 24 percent each call for maximum payments of $1,000 and $2,000. Maximum out-of-pocket expenditures for families range from $600 to $6,000, with $1,500 and $3,000 most prevalent.

A *maximum amount of lifetime coverage* is stated in 91 percent of major medical plans detailing coverage; 25 percent specify a maximum annual amount. Of plans placing maximums on lifetime coverage, 44 percent specify $300,000 or more, 25 percent provide $250,000, 11 percent call for $100,000, and 7 percent pay $50,000. Six plans provide unlimited lifetime major medical coverage. Of plans placing annual maximums on coverage, less than $30,000 is stipulated in 8 percent, $30,000 in 21 percent, $35,000-$75,000 in 33 percent, and $100,000 or more in 38 percent. Thirty-eight percent of the major medical plans permit restoration to maximum coverage after a claim is made.

Employee coverage is paid by the employer under 76 percent of plans that state who will pay for major medical insurance, while the employer and employee share costs under 24 percent.

Coverage for dependents is considered in 97 percent of major medical plans. All clauses specifying the amount of coverage available to dependents state that benefits will be equal to employees' coverage. The cost of dependents' insurance is paid solely by the company under 69 percent of major medical plans that mention costs, while 29 percent state that the employee and the employer will share the cost.

Industry pattern: Major medical coverage is provided in at least two-thirds of plans in lumber, maritime, primary metals, rubber, and stone-clay-glass. Deductibles of $100 per person prevail in electrical machinery, lumber, machinery, maritime, services, and transportation.

Doctors' Visits Benefits

Doctors' visits, both in and out of the hospital, are covered in 29 percent of the insurance plans studied. Of the 96 percent of doctors' visits provisions mentioning in-hospital visits, 18 percent specify a maximum amount payable for total visits. A flat rate for each visit, ranging from $3 to $27, is called for in 29 percent of plans providing in-hospital coverage; a flat rate per day, ranging from $5 to $35, is called for in 24 percent. Eighteen percent limit coverage to reasonable and customary fees.

Out-of-hospital coverage is included in 49 percent of the doctors' visits provisions; 72 percent of these clauses specify that both office visits and house calls will be covered.

Dependents' coverage is equal to employees' coverage under most doctors' visits provisions. In 80 percent of the plans that discuss costs of doctors' visits coverage, the employer pays the full cost of employees' coverage, while in 72 percent the employer pays the cost of dependents' coverage.

Industry pattern: Doctors' visits coverage is included in all surveyed plans in apparel, and in at least one-half of the plans in fabricated metals, foods, furniture, and rubber.

Miscellaneous Medical Expense Benefits

Insurance covering medical expenses not necessarily tied to hospitalization is included in 44 percent of plans in the database. Of plans providing miscellaneous medical expense benefits, almost all (93 percent) cover X-ray and laboratory fees, 49 percent cover anesthetics, and 37 percent cover ambulance costs. Other medical expenses, such as radiation therapy, bandages, prosthetic devices, rental of wheelchairs and other equipment, and oxygen, are provided in 88 percent of these provisions.

Dependent coverage is provided in 97 percent of miscellaneous expense provisions. In all cases dependent coverage is equal to employee coverage. Under most plans specifying who will pay the cost of coverage for employees and dependents, the employer pays.

Industry pattern: Miscellaneous medical expenses are covered in all surveyed plans in apparel and in at least two-thirds of the plans in four other industries: foods, primary metals, rubber, and stone-clay-glass.

Maternity Benefits

Coverage for maternity care is provided in 42 percent of the plans included in the study—44 percent in manufacturing and 37 percent in non-manufacturing. Hospital costs are covered in 71 percent of maternity benefits provisions; surgical costs in 73 percent. More than one-third (38 percent) of the maternity provisions specify that sickness and accident benefits will be paid during absences related to maternity care.

All plans specifying maternity coverage for dependents provide medical coverage equal to that of employees. Of clauses specifying who will pay the cost of employee maternity benefits, 76 percent provide that the employer will pay costs, and the remainder provide that the employer and employee will share costs. Under provisions specifying who will pay the cost of dependent maternity benefits, 69 percent call for the employer to pay costs, 29 percent call for the employer and employee to share costs, and 2 percent call for the employee to pay costs.

Industry pattern: Maternity benefits are found in all surveyed plans in apparel and in at least one-half of the surveyed plans in foods, lumber, machinery, paper, primary metals, rubber, and services.

Comprehensive Insurance

The percentage of comprehensive plans has increased sharply in the last nine years, rising to 48 percent of analyzed plans in this study from 37 percent in 1989, 21 percent in 1986, and only 9 percent in 1983. Comprehensive insurance is found in 47 percent of manufacturing plans (up from 35 percent in 1989, 18 percent in 1986, and 7 percent in 1983) and in 52 percent of non-manufacturing plans (up from 44 percent in 1989, 27 percent in 1986, and 15 percent in 1983).

Of comprehensive plans analyzed, 82 percent specify an initial deductible amount per person before coverage becomes effective. Of these, 25 percent specify a $100 deductible, 23 percent $150, 21 percent $200, and 18 percent more than $200. Of plans mentioning a family deductible, 12 percent specify $200, 32 percent specify $300, and 47 percent specify an amount greater than $300.

Three-quarters of comprehensive plans specifying the amount of coverage provided after the deductible is paid call for 80-20 coinsurance, 14 percent call for 90-10 coinsurance, and 8 percent call for 85-15 coinsurance. Thirty-two percent of the plans permit restoration to maximum coverage after a claim is made.

Seventy-one percent of comprehensive plans specify annual maximum out-of-pocket expenditures per individual, after which the plan pays all costs. Of these, 20 percent call for maximum payments of $1,000, and 48 percent specify payments greater than $1,000. Maximum out-of-pocket expenditures for families range from $200 to $13,500, with $2,000 most prevalent.

A maximum amount of lifetime coverage is stated in 93 percent of comprehensive plans detailing coverage. Only one plan each specifies a maximum amount of coverage per disability or per year. Of plans specifying maximum lifetime coverage, 44 percent specify $1,000,000, 19 percent specify $500,000, and 9 percent specify $750,000. Six plans provide unlimited lifetime comprehensive medical expense coverage.

All comprehensive insurance provisions specifying coverage for dependents provide benefits equal to those of employees. The cost of employee coverage is paid by the employer in 64 percent of comprehensive plans that mention the matter, and is shared by the employer and the employee under 36 percent. Dependent coverage is paid by the employer under 50 percent of these provisions, shared by the employer and employee under 48 percent, and paid by the employee under 2 percent.

Industry pattern: Comprehensive medical coverage is provided in at least one-half of analyzed plans in 13 industries: chemicals, communications, construction, fabricated metals, furniture, insurance and finance, leather, mining, paper, petroleum, printing, textiles, and utilities.

Employee Insurance Benefits

(Frequency Expressed as Percentage of Plans in Each Region*)

	Life Insurance	A D & D	Sickness and Accident	Hospitalization	Surgical	Major Medical	Doctors' Visits	Misc. Medical Expenses	Comprehensive Medical	Dental	Optical
ALL REGIONS	99	72	81	52	52	46	29	44	48	82	43
Middle Atlantic	100	63	81	81	81	76	32	59	20	90	54
Midwest	96	73	86	46	46	41	41	50	55	77	46
New England	92	85	92	46	46	39	23	23	54	69	31
North Central	100	79	91	49	49	46	27	43	51	76	32
Rocky Mountain	100	100	100	25	25	25	25	—	75	75	50
Southeast	96	75	86	36	36	32	18	39	64	64	21
Southwest	100	67	67	17	17	17	17	17	83	100	50
West Coast	100	81	31	56	56	44	44	44	44	100	50
Multiregion	100	56	78	50	50	34	31	50	50	94	66

* See p. xi for area designations.

Coordination of Benefits

Provisions prohibiting duplication of medical benefits provided by other employers, groups, or any government are found in 73 percent of plans surveyed. Non-duplication of benefits provided by other group insurance plans is called for in 134 plans, non-duplication of government provided benefits in 89 plans, and coordination with benefits provided by another employer in 77.

Medical Coverage During Layoff

Continued group health-care coverage during layoffs is stipulated in 56 percent of surveyed plans—64 percent in manufacturing and 35 percent in non-manufacturing. Coverage is extended for periods of time ranging from one month to two-and-one-half years, with three months (19 percent), one year (18 percent), and six months and two years (each 14 percent) mentioned most frequently.

Costs of continued medical coverage during layoff are borne by the employer under 54 percent of clauses providing such coverage, by the employer and employee under 31 percent, and by the employee alone under 15 percent.

Health Care Cost Containment

Provisions designed to lower the cost of health care are found in 79 percent of surveyed plans—80 percent in manufacturing plans and 75 percent in non-manufacturing plans. Most of these measures are intended to reduce costs associated with hospitalization.

Of health care cost containment clauses, 75 percent provide payment for second surgical opinions. Most of these specify payment for a second opinion and for a third opinion if the first two differ. Of second surgical provisions, 70 percent specify that without a second opinion for designated procedures, benefits will be paid at a reduced rate, or not at all. Payment of surgical fees for procedures performed on an outpatient basis at a hospital or at a free-standing facility is specified in 70 percent of plans containing cost-saving provisions.

Provisions designed to reduce the length of hospital stays include coverage for home health care (found in 71 percent of plans with cost containment provisions), coverage for care in a skilled nursing facility (68 percent), and a requirement for pre-admission or utilization review (66 percent).

Other health care cost containment measures found in analyzed plans include a requirement that non-emergency tests be performed on an outpatient basis before admission (59 percent), coverage for hospice care (55 percent), and payment for use of birthing centers (19 percent). Eighteen percent of cost containment provisions restrict weekend admissions, and 14 percent reward employees who detect hospital billing errors.

Over the past six years the number of plans that raised deductibles is a further indication of the drive to cut health care costs. Of major medical plans requiring a deductible, those specifying an amount of more than $100 per person rose from 12 percent in the 1986 study to 21 percent in the 1989 survey and to 24 percent in this year's analysis.

The shift to comprehensive medical plans from traditional hospital-surgical-major medical plans also may be viewed as a move to stem the tide of rising health care costs. Most comprehensive plans require a front-end deductible, payable before any benefits are paid. Under traditional plans, deductibles usually do not apply until after hospital and surgical benefits are exhausted and major medical goes into effect. Further, deductibles under comprehensive plans generally are higher, with 67 percent specifying more than $100 per person, compared with 24 percent of major medical plans.

Premium cost-sharing also has increased significantly over the last six years. The percentage of comprehensive plans requiring workers to share premium costs for individual coverage went to 36 percent this year from 28 percent in the 1989 study and 19 percent in the 1986 survey. Employee contributions are called for in 24 percent of hospital plans discussing financing (up from 22 percent in 1989 and 13 percent in 1986), in 24 percent of surgical plans (up from 21 percent and 12 percent), and in 24 percent of major medical plans (up from 21 percent and 14 percent).

Dental Care

Eighty-two percent of the plans included in this study contain dental insurance, and are found in 77 percent of manufacturing plans and 93 percent of non-manufacturing plans.

Deductibles are specified by 39 percent of dental plans. Of plans requiring a deductible, 50 percent specify $25 and 32 percent specify $50.

Under plans detailing coverage of dental costs, the insurance plan pays a percentage up to a maximum in 72 percent, and according to a schedule up to a maximum in 14 percent. All costs up to a maximum are paid under 5 percent of dental plans.

At least one-half of the dental plans cover X-rays, periodic cleanings and examinations, fillings, extractions, reconstruction (dentures and bridges), endodontics (root canals), periodontia (gum care), and flouride treatments. Orthodontic care is covered in 45 percent of the dental plans.

Coverage is extended to dependents in 94 percent of the plans and is equal to employees' coverage in all cases. Employees' coverage is paid by the company under 80 percent of dental plans that refer to costs and dependents' coverage is paid by the company under 70 percent.

Industry pattern: Dental care is provided in all surveyed plans in chemicals, communications, foods, insurance and finance, maritime, mining, petroleum, printing, and transportation industries, and in at least two-thirds of all other industries except apparel, fabricated metals, furniture, leather, and lumber.

Prescription Drugs

Insurance covering prescription drug costs is included in 47 percent of the sample plans, a climb from 41 percent in the 1989 study, 35 percent in 1986, 29 percent in 1983, and 24 percent in 1979. A deductible is specified in 76 percent of these provisions, and 4 percent state that a percentage of the costs will be paid. Dependent coverage is provided under 95 percent of the prescription drug provisions. All of these clauses provide equal coverage for dependents. Employee and dependent coverage is paid by the employer under most prescription drug provisions.

Industry pattern: Prescription drug benefits are provided in at least one-half of the plans in apparel, fabricated metals, foods, furniture, maritime, paper, printing, retail, rubber, textiles, and transportation equipment.

Optical Care

Insurance covering optical care—including eye examinations, lenses, and frames—is called for in 43 percent of surveyed plans. Optical care is included in 39 percent of manufacturing plans and in 52 percent of non-manufacturing plans.

Coverage is extended to dependents in 91 percent of optical care provisions and is equal to employees' coverage in all cases. In most plans discussing costs of optical insurance, the company pays for both employee and dependent coverage.

Industry pattern: Optical benefits are provided in at least one-half of analyzed plans in 10 industries: apparel, communications, construction, foods, furniture, maritime, primary metals, retail, transportation equipment, and utilities.

Alcohol and Drug Abuse Benefits

Insurance covering treatment of alcohol and drug abuse is included in 58 percent of the sample plans—a climb from 49 percent in the 1989 survey and 32 percent in the 1986 study. This coverage is found in 57 percent of manufacturing agreements, up from 49 percent in 1989 and 30 percent in 1986, and in 60 percent of non-manufacturing contracts, up from 47 percent in 1989 and 38 percent in 1986. Most plans provide coverage for inpatient treatment in a hospital or rehabilitative facility for up to 30 days.

Industry pattern: Insurance covering treatment for alcohol or drug abuse is provided in at least two-thirds of contracts in apparel, communications, construction, foods, leather, maritime, primary metals, services, and transportation equipment.

Medicare-Related Insurance

Insurance coordinating private plans with Medicare benefits is included in 64 percent of the sample plans—67 percent in manufacturing and 56 percent in non-manufacturing. Of these plans 91 percent provide coverage for dependents. Federal law requires employers to offer the same health insurance coverage to workers aged 65 and older as is offered to younger workers, with the option to select either the employer or Medicare as the primary provider. If the employee chooses Medicare, however, the law stipulates that benefits provided under Medicare may not be supplemented by the employer plan.

The company pays the full cost of employees' Medicare-related benefits in 72 percent of plans that mention costs and the full cost of dependent coverage in 70 percent.

Medicare Part B insurance—the optional part of the program that covers physicians' and other medical services—is provided in 29 percent of the sample plans. Of these, 92 percent offer dependent coverage. In most cases the company pays for both employee and dependent coverage.

Industry pattern: Medicare-related insurance is found in at least one-half of the surveyed plans in every industry except electrical machinery, insurance and finance, printing, retail, services, and transportation.

Administration of Insurance Benefits

Administration of insurance plans is discussed in 57 percent of the sample. Of these, 61 percent state that the company is the sole administrator, and 28 percent call for administration by joint company-union trustees. Measures for settling disputes are mentioned in 10 percent of the plans discussing administration; of these 31 percent state that disputes will be resolved jointly by the carrier and the employee, although the company may assist. Under plans discussing settlement of administrative disputes, 62 percent specify that disputes will not be subject to the grievance procedure.

National Health Insurance

Enactment of national health insurance is considered in 20 percent of sample agreements—25 percent in manufacturing and 10 percent in non-manufacturing. Under most of these provisions the parties agree to reopen the bargaining agreement to make any appropriate adjustments required by law. In addition, some contracts contain joint pledges to work together to achieve enactment of national health insurance.

4

Pensions

Almost all contracts included in the Basic Patterns sample make some reference to pension plans. Some agreements simply contain a statement referring to an existing program maintained by the employer or to the amount the employer is required to contribute to a trusteed fund, while others contain fully detailed plans.

Where full detail is stated, a typical plan provides for normal, early, and disability retirement, specifying eligibility requirements and benefits available in each case. Vesting provisions, administrative procedures, and financing arrangements also commonly are covered.

The following analysis is based on 170 plans for which sufficient detail was available. Fifty-one of these plans are multi-employer plans financed by fixed employer contributions.

Normal Retirement

A normal retirement age is specified in all but ten of the 170 available plans. Age 65 is stipulated in 88 percent of these plans; normal retirement ages range from 56 to 62 in the remainder.

A Jan. 1, 1987, amendment to the Age Discrimination in Employment Act outlawed mandatory retirement at age 70, or at any age. If retirement at age 70 was specified in employee benefit plans under collective bargaining contracts in effect June 30, 1986, and terminating after Jan. 1, 1987, the legislation deferred the prohibition of mandatory retirement until expiration of the agreements, or Jan. 1, 1990, whichever occurred first.

Minimum service requirements to become eligible for normal pension benefits are called for in 71 of the available plans. Of these provisions, 42 percent require 10 years of service, and 49 percent require 5 years.

Federal regulations issued pursuant to the above 1987 amendment, prohibit limitations on the number of credited years of service. Collectively bargained plans were given until 1990 to comply.

Service Requirements in Years

(Frequency Expressed as Percentage of 71 Plans Stating Minimums)

Years' Service	1-5	6-10	11-15	16-20	25 or more
Percentage	52	44	—	3	1

Benefit formulas are included in all but seven plans surveyed. Fifty-two percent of benefit formulas guarantee a flat dollar amount a month for each year of service. Under 15 percent of these provisions (mainly in the automobile industry) the monthly amount varies according to base rates or classifications. The monthly flat benefits per year of service range from $4 to $50 (with a median of $20.50). The most common monthly benefits in plans with this formula are $19 per year of service (9 percent), $22 (7 percent), and $18 (6 percent).

In the 1989 survey, the most common benefit was $20 (11 percent), followed by $18 and $17 (each 6 percent), and $16 (5 percent). The median was $18.63.

Number of Plans Providing Flat Monthly Benefit
Per Year of Service

	$5 or less	$5.20-$10	$10.20-$15	$15.20-$20	$20.20 or more
Mfg.	—	2	12	22	29
Non-Mfg.	1	2	—	4	9
All Industries	1	4	12	26	38

Twenty-two of the plans studied compute benefits as a percentage of employees' earnings multiplied by their years of service. Under eight of these, employees' earnings during their entire period of credited service are taken into consideration; in the remaining 14, the percentage is applied to the employee's average earnings during the most recent (or highest paid) period of service—the 10 years preceding retirement, for example.

Under one of the plans, the benefit is the greater of the amounts arrived at under alternative formulas—either a flat dollar amount multiplied by years of service or a percentage of earnings.

In the 51 multi-employer plans included in the study, benefit levels usually are determined by the trustees according to the amount of money in the trust fund. Employees' benefits, commonly stated in a flat amount per month, vary according to their years of service in the industry and the amount of contributions paid into their account.

Four percent of the sample plans integrate Social Security benefits in computing pensions. Cost-of-living adjustments for retirees are found in only three plans studied. Under 17 plans, benefits were increased for retirees.

Contingent annuitant options, whereby an employee may elect to receive a reduced pension which is continued and payable to a spouse or dependent after the employee's death, are specified in all but 13 plans surveyed.

Survivor benefits, payable if an employee dies before reaching normal retirement age, are provided in 90 percent of the plans studied.

Disability Retirement

Pension benefits for employees forced to retire due to total and permanent disability are provided in 88 percent of the plans studied. While 9 percent of disability pension clauses specify a minimum age requirement (50 and 55 being the most common), the majority merely state that an employee must be under normal or early retirement age. Eighty-six percent of disability provisions contain a service requirement—20 percent of these call for 15 years and 61 percent for 10 years.

An eligibility waiting period for disability benefits is imposed in 40 percent of the disability provisions. Under these clauses, the most common waiting period (45 percent) is six months.

Forty-eight percent of the plans specifying amounts of disability pensions employ the same formula used for computing normal benefits. Larger than normal benefits—until the disabled pensioner becomes eligible for normal retirement or social security benefits—are provided in 19 percent of the plans with disability pension formulas. Under 11 percent of the formulas, disability benefits are less than normal benefits.

Grounds for loss of disability benefits are stated in 36 percent of the plans. Of penalty provisions, 43 percent disqualify recipients engaging in any gainful occupation, and 83 percent disqualify those refusing to submit to a medical examination.

Of the 149 plans calling for disability pensions, 48 specify that payments will continue until the retiree is eligible for normal benefits, and 14 state that payments will continue until the retiree is eligible for Social Security benefits.

Disability benefit deductions are mentioned in 36 of the surveyed plans. The most common deductions are social security (11 plans) and workmen's compensation (18 plans).

Industry pattern: All manufacturing plans included in the study contain disability retirement provisions except transportation equipment (93 percent), foods (90 percent), stone-clay-glass (83 percent), paper, rubber, and machinery (each 80 percent), petroleum (75 percent), chemicals (71 percent), textiles (60 percent), and lumber (50 percent). All non-manufacturing plans contain these provisions except retail (92 percent), mining (80 percent), services (77 percent), and communications and utilities (each 67 percent).

Early Retirement

Voluntary early retirement is allowed in 95 percent of the plans. While plans frequently contain several programs for early retirement, this study deals only with typical—age and service—programs.

In 94 percent of plans with early retirement provisions included in this study, an age requirement is specified. Of these, 66 percent stipulate age 55, 16 percent age 60, 10 percent age 62, and 5 percent age 50. A service requirement is stated in 83 percent of early retirement provisions. Under service requirement provisions, the most common requirement is 10 years (59 percent), followed by 15 years (16 percent), five years (13 percent), and 20 years (6 percent).

Benefits usually are proportionately reduced by the number of years an employee is under the normal retirement age. An immediate pension based on credited service at the time of retirement and reduced on the basis of age is called for in 90 percent of early retirement provisions. Twenty-seven percent of early retirement provisions give employees the option of immediate reduced benefits or unreduced benefits at age 65 based on credited service. Twenty-five percent of the provisions studied call for some type of "30 and out" formula permitting retirement after 30 years of service regardless of age.

Industry Pattern: All plans included in the analysis contain voluntary early retirement provisions except foods and machinery (each 90 percent), electrical machinery (89 percent), stone-clay-glass (83 percent), and services (69 percent).

Special early retirement benefits for employees retired by mutual consent or displaced by a plant shutdown or layoff are found in 21 percent of plans contained in this study. Of these provisions, 83 percent permit special early retirement because of plant shutdown, 44 percent by mutual agreement, and 17 percent at employer option.

Age requirements are specified in 47 percent of the special early retirement provisions with age 55 predominating—59 percent, followed by age 50 at 18 percent. Service requirements appear in 64 percent of the provisions with 10 years being the most common (35 percent), followed 15 years (22 percent). Age plus service requirements—whereby an employee's age and years of service combined must total a specified number—are included in 36 percent of special early retirement provisions.

Under 50 percent of plans permitting special early retirement, an employee is entitled to a larger-than-normal benefit which is reduced upon reaching eligibility for normal retirement or Social Security. Larger-than-normal benefits are provided under 17 percent of these provisions, and normal retirement benefits are provided under 8 percent (down from 20 percent in 1989).

Industry pattern: Special early retirement provisions are included mainly in manufacturing plans contained in the database—primary metals 67 percent, transportation equipment 53 percent, and rubber 40 percent.

Vesting

Vesting provisions, under which an employee whose service is terminated remains entitled to earned benefits, are spelled out in 162 of the 170 plans included in this study. Full vesting programs, under which total earned benefits are vested after a maximum 10 years' service, are specified in 146 sample plans. Fifteen plans contain graduated vesting programs, under which accrued benefits initially are partly vested and gradually become fully vested.

Amendments to the Employee Retirement Income Security Act require vesting under one of three formulas beginning Jan. 1, 1989, and by no later than Jan. 1, 1991, for collectively bargained plans. In single-employer plans,

100 percent vesting is required after five years of service or after seven years of service where vesting is graduated. In multi-employer plans, full vesting is required after 10 years for participants covered by collective bargaining agreements.

Portability provisions, which allow employees to change jobs and remain covered by a pension plan and build up credits as long as they work for a contributing employer, appear only in multi-employer plans.

Determination of Credited Service

Under most plans, credited service for pension purposes is divided into two distinct parts—credit for service prior to the effective date of a new or revised plan and credit for service subsequent to the effective date. As a rule, past service is at least equal to seniority as determined under the collective bargaining agreement. In those single-employer plans that define future service, 58 base this computation on continuous service—"continuous service" being roughly equal to seniority. Under another 58 plans, future service is based on the number of hours worked or paid for each year. Of these, the most common hours-worked requirements are 1,000 (40 percent), followed by 1,700 (16 percent), 870 (9 percent), and 1,800 and 600 (each 5 percent). Of the plans with hours requirements, 55 percent give partial credit if the requirement for full credit is not met.

In multi-employer plans, determination of credited service varies, but generally it is based on a combination of number of years' service in the industry and number of hours or days worked for a contributing employer.

Financing and Funding of Pensions

Of the plans for which details are available, 93 percent are non-contributory—that is, entirely financed by the employer. In the remainder costs are shared in varying degrees by employers and employees.

Single-employer contributory plans invariably state exactly how much the employee must contribute, while multi-employer non-contributory plans state how much the employer must contribute. Both contributory and non-contributory single-employer plans, however, are written on the basis of benefits rather than costs. In these, where reference is made to the employer's contribution, the majority stipulate that contributions must be sufficient—as determined by a qualified actuary—to finance the specified benefits.

Funding of pension plan obligations already incurred by setting aside set sums of money in equal annual installments over a prescribed period of time and funding of normal costs for the plan year on a current basis are required by law.

Administration and Termination of Plans

Of the single-employer plans containing administrative procedures, a majority specifies management control, while the remainder specifies joint board control, usually over such matters as procedures and disputes concerning eligibility or applications for pension benefits. All multi-employer plans are jointly administered.

Plan termination is referred to in 66 percent of the plans included in this study. Usually such provisions specify how the existing fund will be distributed among plan participants.

———————

5

Grievances and Arbitration

Grievance and arbitration provisions are found in all 400 contracts contained in CBNC's Basic Patterns database.

Grievance procedures generally follow a relatively standard pattern. Complaints usually are processed through a succession of steps, progressing from lower to higher management and union representatives. In most cases, unresolved disputes proceed through arbitration for resolution by an impartial third party.

Variations occur in the scope of grievance and arbitration systems, the method of presenting and responding to complaints, the number of steps, and the overall complexity of dispute procedures.

Grievance Procedures

Grievance procedures are contained in all of the contracts analyzed.

The scope of the grievance procedure is specified in 91 percent of the sample agreements. Of these, 82 percent permit grievances over any interpretation or application of the contract. In 14 percent of the contracts specifying scope, the grievance procedure encompasses any matter regarding wages, hours, or working conditions. Specific disputes are covered under the grievance procedure in 44 percent of these provisions, while specific complaints are excluded in 29 percent.

Steps In Grievance Procedures

(Frequency Expressed as Percentage of Contracts Specifying Steps)

	Number of Steps				
	1	2	3	4	5
All Industries	9	21	47	21	3
Manufacturing	4	13	53	26	3
Non-manufacturing	17	32	37	12	2

Number of steps is specified in 99 percent of contracts analyzed. Three-step procedures are most common (47 percent), followed by four-step and two-step procedures (each 21 percent), and one-step (9 percent). Five-step systems are outlined in 10 agreements, and six-step systems are called for in one agreement.

First-Step Procedures

Formal first-step procedures are detailed in 96 percent of the sample contracts. Of these, 47 percent give an employee the option of presenting a grievance alone or in the presence of a union representative. Twenty-three percent of first-step procedures state that a grievant will be accompanied by a union representative when presenting a formal grievance, and 19 percent state that grievances are to be presented by a union representative.

Grievances most often are initiated with an employee's immediate supervisor (44 percent of contracts specifying first-step procedures) or with the shop foreman (25 percent).

Manner of first-step presentation is specified in 62 percent of agreements analyzed. Under 54 percent of these provisions, a grievance must be presented in writing, while in the remainder, presentation may be made orally. Management's manner of response is detailed in 42 percent of the sample contracts. In 61 percent of these clauses, a written response is required, and in the rest an oral response is sufficient.

Time limits for filing grievances in the first step vary from one day to six months and appear in 68 percent of contracts studied. Under these provisions, the most common time limits for presenting a grievance to management are five days (21 percent), 30 days (18 percent), 10 days (15 percent), and 15 days (11 percent).

Time limits for management's response at the first step are specified in 54 percent of agreements and vary from one day to 30 days. Management is required to respond after two days in 26 percent of time-limit provisions; after three days in 23 percent; after five days in 18 percent; and after one day in 17 percent. Seven percent of time-limit provisions require a response after 10 days, and 6 percent require a response after seven days.

Union and Management Grievances

Thirty-six percent of sample contracts state that a union may file grievances on its own behalf. These grievances usually deal with management practices or changes affecting a large number of employees or with rights specifically granted to the union under the contract. Management's right to file a grievance is mentioned in 28 percent of the sample.

Industry pattern: Unions are granted access to the grievance machinery in 36 percent each in non-manufacturing and manufacturing agreements. Industries in which at least one-half of contracts permit unions to file grievances on their own behalf include insurance and finance (57 percent) and mining, furniture, printing, and rubber (each 50 percent). At least one-third of the agreements in 10 other industries similarly permit unions to file grievances.

Management is permitted to file grievances in 32 percent of non-manufacturing and 26 percent of manufacturing contracts. Management retains the right to file grievances in 50 percent of printing and rubber industry contracts. In six other industries, an employer's right to initiate grievances is specified in at least one-third of contracts.

Appellate Levels in Grievance Procedures _____

Special requirements for processing complaints beyond the first step in the grievance procedure are included in 86 percent of sample contracts. Of these provisions, 80 percent specify that the grievance must be presented in writing at subsequent steps, 81 percent set time limits for union appeals to higher steps, 82 percent set time limits for management's response, and 69 percent require that management submit a response in writing.

Thirty-six percent of sample contracts specify that if the union or employer fails to respond to a grievance within a specified time limit, the grievance automatically is settled in favor of the other party.

Bypassing of one or more steps or special handling for certain grievances is provided for in 75 percent of the 400 agreements. Under these provisions, grievances most frequently are initiated at a higher step or receive special handling when they concern discharges (82 percent), suspensions (50 percent), general policy or group grievances (30 percent), safety and health issues (15 percent), or grievances filed by management (14 percent). Fifty-two percent of these clauses provide for expedited or special handling for a variety of other disputes, such as grievances over incentive rates and time studies.

Industry pattern: Expedited or special handling of certain grievances is specified in 78 percent of manufacturing and 70 percent of non-manufacturing agreements. This provision is found in at least three-fourths of apparel, electrical machinery, petroleum, transportation, machinery, paper, primary metals, rubber, transportation equipment, mining, maritime, insurance and finance,communications, chemicals, and fabricated metals agreements.

Representatives at mid-level steps are designated in 68 percent of agreements in the database. Most frequently, union representatives handling grievances at mid-level steps are members of an in-company grievance committee (43 percent of these provisions) or shop stewards (18 percent). An international union representative is designated in 4 percent of these clauses, and the local union president is named in 4 percent. Management often is represented at mid-level grievance meetings by industrial relations personnel (27 percent of clauses dealing with the subject) or by the plant manager or the manager's representative (19 percent). In 10 percent of provisions specifying representatives, grievances are handled by a department head, while in 7 percent a foreman handles mid-level grievances.

Joint company/union grievance meetings are provided for in 32 percent of contracts studied. These meetings generally are held to discuss mid-level grievances and are part of the formal grievance procedure. Meetings are scheduled weekly under 17 percent of the contracts calling for joint meetings, monthly under 14 percent, and every two weeks under 9 percent. Eighteen percent of these clauses provide for "regularly scheduled" meetings.

Final-step representatives are specified in 83 percent of agreements. Under these provisions, union representatives at the final step are listed with the following frequency: international representatives (32 percent); in-company grievance committees (24 percent); local presidents (5 percent); and international union presidents (4 percent). Management representatives at the final step most frequently named in provisions dealing with the subject are industrial relations directors (35 percent); plant managers (11 percent); and top executive officers of the company (7 percent).

Union Grievance Representatives

Restrictions are placed on grievance representatives in 41 percent of contracts analyzed, more frequently in manufacturing (54 percent) than in non-manufacturing agreements (21 percent). Of these, 62 percent limit the number of grievance representatives and 13 percent limit the activity of grievance representatives on company time. Twenty-three percent of these clauses place limitations on both the number and activity of representatives.

Special job security provisions (not superseniority) are included in 33 percent of agreements studied. Forty-four percent of these contracts prohibit management from discriminating against grievance representatives or interfering with their activities, and 44 percent grant shift- overtime- or holiday work-preference for union representatives.

Industry pattern: Special job security provisions for grievance representatives are included in 33 percent of manufacturing and 34 percent of non-manufacturing contracts. At least one-half of contracts in the textiles, furniture, machinery, transportation equipment, and construction industries provide some form of job security to grievance representatives. Further, at least one-third of retail, utilities, and electrical machinery agreements contain such clauses.

Pay for union representatives who present, investigate, or handle grievances is mentioned in 53 percent of contracts in the database. The number of hours for which management pays grievance representatives is limited in 19 percent of these clauses. Twenty-four percent of contracts dealing with the subject contain a general statement that paid time will not be "unreasonable or excessive."

Industry pattern: Pay provisions for union grievance investigators are included in 67 percent of manufacturing agreements and in 32 percent of non-manufacturing contracts. Compensation is granted to grievance representatives in all contracts in the rubber and furniture industries, and in at least three-fourths of contracts in machinery, petroleum, electrical machinery, leather, transportation equipment, and chemicals. More than one-half of contracts in textiles, primary metals, paper, fabricated metals, stone-clay-glass, communications, and utilities specify pay for grievance procedure activity.

Conciliation and Mediation _____

Only 13 of the 400 sample contracts call for conciliation and/or mediation. Under 11 of these agreements, conciliation/mediation is an intermediate step between grievance and arbitration; under the remaining two, it is the final step in the grievance procedure.

Arbitration _____

Arbitration is called for in 99 percent of the sample contracts—100 percent in manufacturing and 97 percent in non-manufacturing.

Industry pattern: Arbitration provisions appear in all contracts in all industries with the exception of construction (97 percent), retail (96 percent), transportation (92 percent), and lumber (86 percent).

The scope of arbitration is specified in 95 percent of the sample. Of these provisions, 93 percent provide for arbitration of any dispute not resolved through the grievance procedure. Specific issues are excluded from arbitration procedures in 35 percent of these contracts; specific issues are included in 29 percent. In 5 percent of provisions specifying scope of arbitration, certain matters bypass the grievance procedure and go directly to arbitration.

Initiation procedures are described in 98 percent of the contracts studied. Of these provisions, 90 percent state that arbitration may be invoked at the request of either party; 10 percent stipulate that arbitration automatically follows the grievance procedure. Mutual agreement of the parties is required to proceed to arbitration under less than 1 percent of initiation clauses.

Time limits on appealing a grievance to arbitration are included in 76 percent of the 400 contracts and range from one day to six months. Under these provisions, the most frequently designated time limits are 30 days (30 percent), 10 days (19 percent), 15 days (11 percent), five days (10 percent), 20 days (5 percent), and seven days (4 percent).

Selection of Arbitrator

(Frequency Expressed as Percentage of Contracts Specifying Selection)

Selection Process	All Industries	Manufacturing	Non-manufacturing
Single Arbitrator Appointed by Contract	5	7	2
Permanent Board Appointed by Contract	1	1	1
List of Arbitrators, Serving on Rotating Basis	6	7	5
Ad Hoc, Selected by Parties	45	43	49
Ad Hoc, via Facilities of Impartial Party	28	30	26

Selection of an arbitrator is detailed in 97 percent of the agreements analyzed. In 45 percent of the contracts specifying a method of selection, the arbitrator is chosen on an ad hoc basis by the parties, and in 28 percent, the arbitrator is selected on an ad hoc basis through the facilities of an impartial agency (generally from a list of arbitrators supplied by the agency). Under 7 percent of selection clauses, a permanent arbitration board is appointed, or a list of arbitrators, who serve on a rotating basis, is included in the agreement. A single arbitrator is appointed to serve for the duration of the contract in 5 percent of the provisions.

Under 53 percent of contracts specifying the selection process, an impartial agency is used to select the arbitrator if the parties reach an impasse in the selection process or if the chosen arbitrator is unavailable. The Federal Mediation and Conciliation Service is the impartial agency used in 60 percent of these clauses, followed by the American Arbitration Association (29 percent). Eleven percent of these provisions specify other impartial agencies, including state or federal courts, or state mediation agencies.

The number of arbitrators is specified in 96 percent of the sample agreements. In 82 percent of these contracts the services of a single arbitrator are employed, while in 13 percent, three arbitrators (usually an impartial chairman selected by one arbiter chosen by management and one chosen by the union) are specified. Five percent of agreements indicating the number of arbiters call for a five-member arbitration board.

Industry pattern: Of contracts discussing the number of arbitrators, a majority of manufacturing (90 percent) and non-manufacturing (67 percent) contracts specify a single arbiter. All agreements in the paper, fabricated metals, mining, apparel, stone-clay-glass, and leather industries call for a single arbitrator. In addition, all but one of the contracts in the maritime, electrical machinery, machinery, rubber, furniture, lumber, and textiles industries call for one arbiter. At least 50 percent of petroleum, transportation, and utilities industry contracts specify three-member arbitration boards.

Determination of arbitrability of a dispute is addressed in only 41 of the sample agreements. In all but 11 of these contracts, the decision as to whether a dispute is properly before an arbitrator is left to the arbiter selected to hear the case.

Restrictions are placed on arbitrators in 83 percent of agreements studied. Of these, 93 percent apply a general restriction prohibiting the arbitrator from adding to, subtracting from, or in any way altering contract language. Twenty-five percent of restrictive clauses specify that arbitrators must submit their decisions in writing, and 40 percent require that decisions be rendered within a specified time period, usually 30 days.

Retroactivity of an arbitrator's award is mentioned in 34 percent of agreements in the database. Of these, 47 percent limit retroactivity to a specified point prior to the filing of the grievance, 16 percent limit retroactivity to the point of filing the grievance, and 4 percent limit retroactivity to the point of occurrence of the action giving rise to the grievance.

Arbitration expenses are mentioned in 92 percent of the sample. Under 90 percent of these provisions, the fee is shared equally by the parties. Where a multiple-member arbitration board is used, the parties generally assume the costs of their own representatives on the board, and share the fee of the impartial chairman. In 5 percent of expense clauses, the fee is paid by the losing party.

Collateral expenses (for example, copies of transcripts of arbitration hearings) are discussed in 29 percent of contracts containing arbitration expense provisions. Under 44 percent of these clauses, costs are shared equally, and under 40 percent, the costs are paid by the party requesting transcripts or other services.

Seventeen percent of expense provisions refer to pay for time lost by witnesses at an arbitration hearing; most provide for reimbursement by the calling party.

Grievance and Arbitration Provisions

(Frequency Expressed as Percentage of Contracts in Each Region*)

	All Regions	Middle Atlantic	Midwest	New England	North Central	Rocky Mountain	Southeast	Southwest	West Coast	Multiregion
Grievance Procedure	100	100	100	100	100	100	100	100	100	100
Scope of Grievance Procedure	91	94	93	85	92	70	92	100	93	89
Union May File	36	38	36	35	32	30	26	46	38	46
Company May File	28	32	32	35	22	30	21	39	29	31
Restrictions on Grievance Reps	41	34	39	35	45	20	53	77	36	37
Job Security For Grievance Reps	33	42	25	23	40	40	28	23	29	27
Pay For Investigation	53	51	43	54	67	40	62	85	18	52
Conciliation	3	5	7	–	4	–	4	–	2	–
Arbitration	99	98	96	100	100	100	100	100	98	98
Scope of Arbitration	95	95	93	100	96	90	96	100	89	94
Restrictions on Arbitrators	83	81	71	81	84	100	94	85	82	81
Arbitration Expenses	92	85	93	89	98	90	94	92	91	92

* See p. xi for area designations.

6

Income Maintenance

Income maintenance provisions are found in 53 percent of the Basic Patterns database sample. The three major types of income protection are work or pay guarantees, severance pay, and supplemental unemployment benefit plans. Geographic analysis shows that income maintenance guarantees are most common in Middle Atlantic region and multiregion contracts.

Trend in Income Maintenance Provisions

(Frequency Expressed as Percentage of Contracts)

	1966	1971	1975	1979	1983	1986	1989	1992
Income main-tenance	38	40	48	49	51	52	52	53
Work or pay guarantees	6	5	6	9	11	13	13	13
Severance	29	34	39	37	39	41	40	40
SUB *	14	15	17	16	16	16	14	14

* SUB percentages include unavailable plans.

Guarantees of Work or Pay

Work or pay guarantees are called for in 53 contracts. Of the 38 contracts calling for weekly guarantees, 25 guarantee 40 hours per week, nine call for 35 hours to 38 hours, one calls for 32 hours, and one provides for 15 hours. Two agreements specify a minimum amount of weekly pay, without reference to hours. In seven contracts the weekly guarantee is reduced during holiday weeks.

Monthly guarantees appear in two agreements. One provides a certain number of hours of work or pay per month, and one guarantees a percentage of average monthly pay. Three contracts in the study provide annual guarantees of 1,400 hours to 2,080 hours. Also contained in the sample are four contracts guaranteeing employment for the term of the agreement, and three contracts specifying a lifetime guarantee. A variety of long-term guarantees, guaranteed annual income streams for high-seniority workers, and guarantees of work or pay for jobs lost to subcontracting, are found in the three major auto industry contracts.

Nearly three-fifths (59 percent) of work or pay guarantees cover all regular employees; more than one-quarter require a minimum amount of service. Guarantees may be voided under 51 percent of these contracts, generally in the event of a strike, lack of work for reasons beyond an employer's control, acts of God, or time absent without cause.

Industry pattern: Guarantees appear in 7 percent of contracts in manufacturing and in 23 percent of agreements in non-manufacturing. Twelve guarantee provisions are found in retail, 11 in transportation, nine in foods, five in services, four in maritime, three in transportation equipment, two each in printing and utilities, and one each in construction, electrical machinery, insurance and finance, primary metals, and textiles.

Weekly guarantees are concentrated in foods, retail, services, and transportation. Two agreements in transportation contain monthly guarantees. Annual guarantees are found in two maritime agreements and one utilities agreement. Lifetime guarantees appear in two printing contracts and one transportation agreement. Guarantees for the life of the contract are found in retail (two agreements), electrical machinery, and transportation equipment (each one).

Severance Pay

Severance or separation pay, provided for under 40 percent of the sample, may be awarded in a lump sum either upon termination, or after a specified period of time, or in installments. These provisions are found in 45 percent of manufacturing contracts and in 34 percent of non-manufacturing agreements. Although many severance pay clauses are part of SUB plans, they are treated separately in this section.

Employees terminated as a result of a permanent shutdown are eligible for severance pay under 50 percent of severance plans studied. Severance is payable to employees on layoff for a minimum length of time in 16 percent of the provisions; to employees on layoff with no prospect of recall in 17 percent; and to employees on any layoff or on layoff for unspecified reasons in 24 percent. Three percent of these plans call for severance pay at retirement, and 11 percent provide severance for employees who are ineligible for pensions. Severance is payable for other reasons under 29 percent of the provisions.

The most common method for determining the amount of severance benefit—found in 80 percent of severance provisions—is a schedule based on service and earnings. Almost two-thirds (66 percent) of provisions basing severance on service and earnings call for graduated schedules that increase the number of weeks' pay as length of service increases. The remainder provide a specific number of weeks' pay per year of service. Of those providing a specific number of weeks' pay for each year of service, 77 percent call for one week's pay, 12 percent provide one-half week's pay, and 3 percent provide two weeks' pay (the maximum amount found in this study).

Six percent of severance provisions pay a flat weekly sum per year of service. While weekly pay ranges from $30 to $400 a week per year of service, the most common amount is $100. Under 7 percent of severance plans studied, pay is based solely on earnings.

Limitations on the duration of severance pay are imposed in 50 percent of severance provisions and range from two to 104 weeks. The most common limit is eight weeks, appearing in 20 percent of limitations. Following in frequency are limitations of 52 weeks (16 percent), 10 weeks (11 percent) and four weeks (8 percent).

Income Maintenance Provisions

(Frequency Expressed as Percentage of Industry Contracts)

	Income Main-tenance Provision	Work or Pay Guarantee	Severance	SUB*
ALL INDUSTRIES	53	13	40	14
MANUFACTURING	54	7	45	20
Apparel	—	—	—	—
Chemicals	69	—	69	6
Electrical Machinery	70	5	65	25
Fabricated Metals	47	—	37	32
Foods	86	43	67	5
Furniture	17	—	17	—
Leather	50	—	50	—
Lumber	—	—	—	—
Machinery	46	—	38	15
Paper	57	—	57	—
Petroleum	71	—	71	—
Primary Metals	64	4	40	48
Printing	88	25	75	13
Rubber	50	—	50	50
Stone-Clay-Glass	31	—	31	15
Textiles	20	10	10	—
Transportation Equipment	62	9	41	44
NON-MANUFACTURING	50	23	34	4
Communications	100	—	100	—
Construction	7	3	3	3
Insurance & Finance	43	14	29	—
Maritime	63	50	13	13
Mining	42	—	33	25
Retail	81	44	56	4
Services	44	19	26	—
Transportation	64	44	40	—
Utilities	30	20	20	—

* Includes plans not available for analysis in this study.

A minimum service requirement is found in 85 percent of severance pay plans. One year of service is stipulated by 46 percent of minimum service provisions; two years and three years each by 16 percent; five years by 7 percent; and six months by 5 percent.

Restrictions on receipt of benefits are imposed in 58 percent of severance pay plans. Forty-six percent of these clauses deny benefits if employees refuse other work; one-third deny benefits to employees if they are eligible for a pension. Nearly one-third (32 percent) of agreements placing limitations on receipt of benefits state that workers who quit are ineligible for severance pay. Benefits are denied for various other reasons under 66 percent of these restrictions.

Reemployment after receipt of severance benefits is mentioned in 39 percent of plans studied. Repayment of severance benefits is not required under 26 percent of provisions discussing such reemployment; a repayment obligation is removed after a specified time under 5 percent. Almost one-third (31 percent) of these clauses state that seniority earned before layoff will not be reinstated.

Financing is discussed—often under SUB financing provisions—in 12 percent of severance pay plans. Of severance provisions mentioning financing, 90 percent require the company to bear all costs, and 60 percent place some limit on the company's obligation.

Industry pattern: Severance pay provisions appear in every agreement in communications and in at least one-half of contracts in chemicals, electrical machinery, foods, leather, paper, petroleum, printing, retail, and rubber. Severance provisions are absent from all surveyed agreements in apparel, and lumber and are found in only one contract each in construction, furniture, maritime, and textiles.

Supplemental Unemployment Benefits _____

Fifty-six of the 400 sample contracts make some reference to supplemental unemployment benefit plans. In this study, all such plans are referred to as SUB plans. No text or descriptive material is available for 14 of these plans. Therefore, the working sample in the following analysis consists of 42 plans for which sufficient detail was available.

SUB plans fall into two categories: pooled fund systems and individual account plans. Pooled fund systems provide benefits only in the event of lack of work. Under individual account plans, employees have a vested right to their accounts and may withdraw the full amount at termination. Individual account plans sometimes impose a maximum for each account and limit the amount employees may withdraw each week. Some of these plans allow employees to withdraw money from the account for reasons other than layoff and termination. Only six individual account plans appear in the present study.

Industry pattern: Of the 56 SUB plans (including those that were unavailable), 15 are in transportation equipment and 12 are in primary metals. Six plans are found in fabricated metals, five in electrical machinery, and four in machinery. Three plans each are found in mining and rubber, two are in stone-clay-glass, and one each appears in chemicals, construction, foods, maritime, printing, and retail.

Income Maintenance Provisions, By Region

(Frequency Expressed as Percentage of Contracts in Each Region*)

	Income Maintenance Provision	Work or Pay Guarantee	Severance	SUB**
Middle Atlantic	57	15	48	10
Midwest	39	11	32	4
Northeast	46	12	31	8
North Central	54	12	43	13
Rocky Mountain	50	20	30	—
Southeast	47	9	34	11
Southwest	31	8	23	8
West Coast	40	16	22	7
Multiregion	77	17	60	44

* See p. xi for area designation.
** Includes plans not available for analysis in this study.

Among unions in the study that negotiated SUB plans are the United Auto Workers with 19 plans in the sample and the United Steelworkers with 17 plans. The International Association of Machinists, International Brotherhood of Electrical Workers, and United Rubber Workers each agreed to three plans. The Aluminum, Brick and Glass Workers International Union, International Union of Electronic Workers, and International Union of Operating Engineers were party to two plans each. The other unions in the sample—each represented by one plan—are the Allied Industrial Workers; Bakery, Confectionery and Tobacco Workers; Chemical Workers International Union; United Food and Commercial Workers; Graphic Communications International Union; Metal Trades Council; Plumbers and Pipefitters; and Seafarers' International Union.

Full week benefits are computed by a variety of methods. One of the most common methods of computation, found in 12 plans, is payment of an amount equal to a percentage of an employee's take-home pay, with the amount of weekly unemployment compensation (UC) usually deducted. Seven of these provisions (five in transportation equipment and two in machinery) pay an amount which, when added to an employee's unemployment compensation, equals 95 percent of take-home pay minus $12.50 or $17.50 in work-related expenses not incurred. The percentage of take-home pay in the other five plans ranges from 60 percent to 100 percent.

Another common computation method, payment of a multiple of an employee's hourly rate (usually minus UC), also occurs in 12 plans and is found most often in primary metals. Seven of these pay 26 times an employee's hourly rate, four pay multiples of 28, and one pays a multiple of 37.5.

Seven SUB plans pay a percentage of straight time pay (minus UC). Three rubber plans pay 80 percent of straight time pay, one plan in fabricated metals pays 95 percent, one in transportation equipment pays 70 percent, one in machinery pays 62 percent, and one in electrical machinery pays 60 percent. Other methods of calculating payment include a percentage of an employee's individual account and various amounts based on an employee's job classification.

In most plans that describe the amount of full-week benefits, the amount is affected by receipt of unemployment compensation.

Maximum payments are specified in 25 plans. Eight of these plans state a flat weekly maximum. These maximums are: $75, $90, $150, $260, and $336.

Another eight plans (mostly in primary metals) provide two maximums: one for weeks in which employees receive UC benefits and one for weeks in which they do not. These two maximums are $100 and $150 in one plan and $180 and $235 in the remaining seven.

Seven plans (mostly in transportation equipment) state a maximum only for weeks in which an employee is no longer receiving UC and/or has refused an offer of work. The stipulated maximums are $50 in one plan, $100 in two, $115 in two, $135 in one, and $150 in one.

Minimum payments are specified in nine plans analyzed. In seven of these, $2 week is the minimum payment. Other minimums found are $10 and $258.

Dependents' allowances are added to full-week benefits in 13 plans (mostly in primary metals). The amount is $1.50 per dependent under all but two of the plans. One plan adds $2.50 per dependent and one plan $3. All plans limit the allowance to four dependents.

Duration of benefits is discussed in 35 plans. A majority (71 percent) of these cancel credit units for each week an employee receives benefits; others link duration directly to seniority (46 percent) and/or to the condition of the trust fund (54 percent). In plans using credit units, employees generally accrue a specified number of credit units per week or per pay period, up to a maximum. When an employee begins to collect benefits, credit units are cancelled. The number of credit units cancelled per benefit often depends on the condition of the SUB trust fund and an employee's seniority.

A typical plan using credit units states that an employee, after attaining one year of seniority, will accrue one-half credit unit per week up to a maximum of 52 credit units. When an employee begins to draw benefits, the number of credit units cancelled per benefit depends on the condition of the trust fund. When the fund is at its highest level, one credit unit per benefit is cancelled, regardless of seniority—thus the maximum is computed as 52 weeks. When fund levels drop, a greater number of credit units are cancelled per benefit, depending on seniority. As many as 10 credit units per benefit may be cancelled for employees with limited seniority when a fund reaches a low level. When funds drop below a specified level, benefit payments cease completely.

Some plans basing duration on credit units cancel a fixed number of credit units per benefit but reduce the amount of benefit when a trust fund falls below a certain level.

A maximum duration is stated in 25 plans. Under 11 plans, the maximum is 104 weeks and under 8 plans, 52 weeks. In each of two plans maximums are four years and five years. Other maximums, appearing in only one agreement each, are 26 weeks and 39 weeks. In most cases maximums of more than 52 weeks apply only to workers with long service.

Seniority requirements for SUB eligibility are found in 31 plans. One year is the requirement in 15 plans, and two years is specified in 12 plans. The remaining plans require 25 months, four years, five years, or 20 years of seniority.

Most of the plans studied deny payment of SUB for layoffs resulting from a labor dispute (33 contracts), those of a disciplinary nature (32 contracts), or those caused by circumstances beyond an employer's control such as a civil riot or natural disaster (27 contracts).

Employee obligations that have become a standard part of most SUB plans include the following: receipt or eligibility to receive unemployment compensation (32 agreements); duty to apply for benefits (26 agreements); acceptance of company offer of other work (24 plans); acceptance of suitable work offered by the state unemployment service (23 agreements).

Of the 32 plans requiring that an employee receive or be eligible to receive unemployment compensation, 31 state exceptions to this rule. Exceptions include: exhaustion of UC rights (29 plans); an insufficient period of work under a state system to qualify for a benefit (27 plans); receipt of other compensation disqualifying an employee for UC benefits (26 plans); a second waiting week under a state system (24 plans); receipt of disability or retirement benefits an employee could have received while at work or participation in a federal training program (15 plans each); rejection of a company work offer as allowed by the contract (13 plans); or a benefit denial contrary to the intent of the plan (11 plans). Other exceptions are found in 24 plans.

Short workweek benefits are available under 27 of the SUB plans. In 12 each of these provisions, hours worked under 40 and hours worked under 32 serve as the basis of payment. One contract uses a 30-hour base. Benefits are computed as the number of unworked hours times 80 percent of straight-time pay in 11 of the provisions, and times 100 percent in another 11. Under the remaining four of these clauses, the amount paid varies according to seniority. Eligibility requirements generally are the same as for full-week benefits, and most plans state that short workweek benefits will be paid automatically without employee application.

Financing is mentioned in 31 of sample pooled-fund plans. Usually an employer contributes a certain amount per hour worked; in 25 of these plans an employer's obligation ceases after the SUB fund reaches a specified maximum.

7

Hours and Overtime

Hours and overtime provisions are found in all but three of the 400 contracts in CBNC's Basic Patterns database. All manufacturing contracts contain these provisions. In non-manufacturing, two insurance and finance agreements and one transportation agreement omit them. Geographic analysis of the sample shows hours and overtime provisions appear in all contracts in all regions except the Mid-Atlantic (99 percent), multiregion (96 percent), and West Coast (93 percent) agreements.

Typical clauses include daily and weekly work schedules, requirements for overtime premiums, regulations for the distribution of overtime work, length of lunch and rest periods, and rules governing pay for time lost on a day of injury or for time spent traveling to and from work.

Work Schedules

Daily work schedules are specified in 85 percent of contracts studied. Of these, 94 percent call for an eight-hour day and 5 percent provide for a standard workday of less than eight hours. Two contracts call for workdays of more than eight hours.

Industry pattern: Less than eight-hour workdays are specified in 5 percent of manufacturing and in 3 percent of non-manufacturing industry agreements. These provisions predominate in apparel with 67 percent of the contracts specifying a daily work schedule of seven and one-half hours or less.

Weekly work schedules are spelled out in 65 percent of the sample. Of these, the majority (94 percent) provide a normal workweek of 40 hours; the remainder specify workweeks ranging from 35 hours to 39.5 hours.

Industry pattern: Provisions for less than 40-hour workweeks appear in 4 percent of manufacturing and in 3 percent of non-manufacturing agreements. Shorter workweeks are specified in 78 percent of apparel agreements; the remainder are scattered throughout the sample.

Five-day workweeks are specified in 57 percent of contracts; 40 percent of sample contracts call for a Monday-through-Friday schedule.

Scheduling of Work

Work scheduling is a management prerogative under 52 percent of contracts included in the database—54 percent in manufacturing and 49 percent in non-manufacturing. Sixty-three percent of the sample contracts discuss work schedule changes. These provisions appear in 68 percent of manufacturing agreements and 56 percent of non-manufacturing contracts. Of the change in work schedules clauses, 40 percent require notification to or discussion with the union; 32 percent require union agreement.

Overtime Work

Nearly all agreements studied (97 percent) provide premium pay for overtime work. These provisions are found in 99 percent of manufacturing agreements and in 93 percent of non-manufacturing contracts.

Daily overtime premiums are provided in 92 percent of agreements. Of these, 92 percent require overtime pay after eight hours' work and 4 percent provide premium pay after less than eight hours. Provisions calling for overtime premiums after seven or seven and one-half hours' work predominate in apparel and printing agreements. Work before or after the regular daily schedule is paid at the overtime rate under 29 percent of sample contracts.

Daily overtime rates are specified in 92 percent of agreements. Nearly all of these provisions call for time and one-half; one calls for doubletime.

Under 26 percent of sample agreements, a doubletime premium is paid after a specified number of hours beyond the daily schedule have been worked at a time and one-half rate. This type of premium pay appears more frequently in manufacturing contracts (30 percent) than in non-manufacturing contracts (19 percent). Of these clauses, 58 percent pay doubletime after four hours of overtime work; 19 percent after two hours; 13 percent after eight hours.

Weekly overtime pay provisions are stipulated in 72 percent of agreements—74 percent in manufacturing and 69 percent in non-manufacturing. Of these, 94 percent pay time and one-half after 40 hours' work, while 5 percent pay overtime for less than 40 hours' work (mainly in the apparel industry).

Sixth-day premiums are called for in 23 percent of contracts—25 percent in manufacturing and 20 percent in non-manufacturing. All of these agreements provide time and one-half pay for work on the sixth day. A requirement that the sixth day be the sixth consecutive day of work in order to qualify for overtime pay is found in 45 percent of the clauses.

Seventh-day premiums are paid in 26 percent of contracts—30 percent in manufacturing and 21 percent in non-manufacturing. Of these, 83 percent call for doubletime rates and 61 percent contain a "consecutive day" requirement.

Layoffs to avoid weekly overtime are prohibited under 25 percent of agreements—26 percent in manufacturing and 23 percent in non-manufacturing. These prohibitions are found in 71 percent of petroleum, 67 percent of mining, 57 percent each of lumber and paper, 56 percent of chemicals, 54 percent of stone-clay-glass, and 50 percent of utilities agreements.

Pyramiding of overtime pay is prohibited in 66 percent of contracts in the database—74 percent in manufacturing and 52 percent in non-manufacturing. Under such provisions, neither payment of both daily and weekly overtime for the same hours of work nor more than one type of premium for any one day (holiday pay plus doubletime on seventh day worked, for example) is allowed. In 20 of the 26 industries studied, at least half of the agreements contain pyramiding provisions.

Hours and Overtime Provisions

(Frequency Expressed as Percentage of Contracts in Each Region*)

	All Regions	Middle Atlantic	Midwest	New England	North Central	Rocky Mountain	Southeast	Southwest	West Coast	Multiregion
Work Schedule Provisions	95	98	100	100	97	100	96	92	93	83
Schedule Specified										
Daily	85	83	82	96	87	90	87	92	84	79
Weekly	65	57	71	85	65	80	60	85	73	52
Monday thru Friday	40	43	43	42	37	40	34	39	56	31
Overtime Pay Provisions	97	98	100	96	99	100	100	100	96	87
Premium Pay for										
Daily OT	92	93	96	96	96	80	89	92	89	83
Weekly OT	72	70	71	73	75	80	89	85	60	60
Sixth Day OT	23	20	36	15	22	20	30	8	20	27
Seventh Day OT	26	21	32	15	23	—	45	15	24	37
Saturday OT	51	50	57	62	68	40	28	46	51	39
Sunday OT	63	62	68	65	76	70	49	69	56	50
Layoffs to Avoid Prohibited	25	23	14	15	28	20	36	39	13	29
Pyramiding Prohibited	66	66	71	65	74	60	75	54	44	60
Advance Notice Required	29	34	29	19	39	30	19	15	11	33
Distribution Procedures	66	67	68	58	78	40	68	85	44	62

* See p. xi for area designations.

Distribution of overtime work is discussed in 70 percent of the sample—82 percent of manufacturing agreements and 52 percent of non-manufacturing contracts. A general statement to the effect that overtime will be equally distributed as far as practical or possible is contained in 66 percent of distribution provisions.

Procedures for the distribution of overtime work are defined in 66 percent of the sample and are far more common in manufacturing (76 percent) than in non-manufacturing (51 percent) contracts. Of the distribution procedure clauses, 38 percent spread overtime equally among all employees; 21 percent assign overtime on a strict seniority basis; 14 percent provide for cumulative equalization of overtime; and 9 percent distribute overtime by rotating assignments.

Of the agreements containing overtime distribution procedures, 55 percent limit assignments to employees within a job classification; 44 percent to employees within a department; 34 percent to employees qualified to do the job; and 26 percent each to employees who normally perform the work and to employees on a particular shift.

Posting of overtime records is required under 18 percent of agreements. Records must be made available to the union under 19 percent of the contracts analyzed. Eight percent of sample contracts specify that disputes over distribution of overtime are subject to the grievance procedure.

Acceptance of overtime work is discussed in 30 percent of the 400 agreements. In 47 percent of these provisions, overtime is mandatory; in 40 percent it is voluntary; in 13 percent it is voluntary except in case of emergency. Of the 24 percent of contracts imposing penalties for refusal of overtime work, nearly all (92 percent) specify a loss of claim to the number of hours refused. A penalty for not reporting for accepted overtime is contained in 10 percent of the sample.

Restrictions on overtime assignments are imposed in 44 percent of sample contracts—55 percent in manufacturing and 25 percent in non-manufacturing. Under 66 percent of these provisions, advance notice (or advance notice except in case of emergency) of overtime assignments is required. Failure to give advance notice relieves employees of the obligation to work overtime under 18 percent of agreements discussing restrictions. Overtime is prohibited during periods of layoff in 5 percent of contracts containing restrictions, and a maximum is placed on the amount of overtime allowed in 31 percent.

Premium Pay for Weekend Work

A premium rate is paid for weekend work under 67 percent of sample contracts in the database. Weekend premiums are provided in 78 percent of manufacturing agreements and 49 percent of non-manufacturing agreements.

Premium pay for work on Saturday as such is called for in 51 percent of surveyed contracts. The standard premium rate is time and one-half, although 10 percent of the sample pays doubletime after a given number of hours' work (most often eight). Less than 2 percent of agreements specifying Saturday premiums provide for doubletime for all Saturday work.

Industry pattern: Saturday premiums are found in twice the percentage of manufacturing (64 percent) contracts as in non-manufacturing (32 percent) contracts. Such provisions appear most frequently in machinery (96 percent), fabricated metals (89 percent), electrical machinery (85 percent), and construction and transportation equipment (each 79 percent) agreements.

Premium pay for work on Sunday as such is required in 63 percent of contracts. Doubletime pay, the most common premium for Sunday work, is provided under 78 percent of these agreements; 21 percent pay time and one-half. Three of these provisions call for time and one-quarter, and one calls for tripletime.

Industry pattern: Sunday premiums are paid under 75 percent of manufacturing agreements and 44 percent of non-manufacturing agreements. They are found in all leather and furniture contracts; in 96 percent of machinery contracts; in 93 percent of construction agreements; in 90 percent of electrical machinery contracts; and in more than three-fourths of those in fabricated metals, rubber, textiles, and transportation equipment industries.

Of sample contracts specifying premium pay for Sunday work, doubletime prevails in chemicals, construction, electrical machinery, fabricated metals, foods, furniture, insurance and finance, machinery, paper, printing, rubber, textiles, and transportation equipment.

Overtime Provisions

(Frequency Expressed as Percentage of Contracts in Each Industry)

	Provisions	PREMIUM PAY FOR						Layoffs to Avoid Prohibited	Pyramiding Prohibited	Advance Notice Required	Distribution Procedures
		Daily OT	Weekly OT	6th Day OT	7th Day OT	Saturday OT	Sunday OT				
ALL INDUSTRIES	97	92	72	23	26	51	63	25	66	29	66
MANUFACTURING	99	95	74	25	30	64	75	26	74	40	76
Apparel	100	89	33	11	22	67	22	—	11	56	22
Chemicals	100	100	94	38	63	50	63	56	100	25	88
Elec. Machinery	100	100	50	30	35	85	90	15	65	65	90
Fab. Metals	100	100	84	16	16	89	84	26	74	63	84
Foods	100	100	90	33	33	62	71	24	67	43	71
Furniture	100	100	83	17	17	67	100	17	83	83	67
Leather	100	100	75	25	25	75	100	—	75	75	50
Lumber	100	86	100	14	14	29	43	57	71	14	71
Machinery	100	100	69	15	19	96	96	23	88	58	88
Paper	93	93	79	7	—	36	57	57	79	14	57
Petroleum	100	100	100	14	57	—	43	71	86	29	86
Primary Metals	100	96	84	52	56	52	68	28	84	24	68
Printing	100	63	25	—	—	50	63	—	25	38	50
Rubber	100	100	67	17	—	50	83	17	100	17	67
Stone, Clay, & Glass	100	92	85	15	38	23	69	54	77	15	69
Textiles	100	90	80	40	50	60	80	—	70	—	70
Trans. Equip.	97	91	59	24	24	79	85	6	74	41	91
NON-MANUFACTURING	93	86	69	20	21	32	44	23	52	12	51
Communications	100	90	80	10	10	20	50	20	90	20	80
Construction	97	97	34	—	—	79	93	—	10	3	24
Insurance & Finance	71	43	57	—	—	71	57	14	29	—	43
Maritime	88	75	38	—	—	50	50	—	25	—	25
Mining	100	92	100	33	50	17	17	67	92	25	75
Retail	96	93	93	44	19	19	56	15	59	7	41
Services	100	81	93	37	52	22	19	33	70	15	56
Transportation	76	76	48	12	16	4	4	28	44	20	60
Utilities	100	100	90	10	20	10	50	50	70	10	90

Lunch, Rest, and Cleanup Provisions _____

Lunch periods are referred to in 65 percent of the sample contracts. Such provisions appear in 56 percent of manufacturing and 79 percent of non-manufacturing contracts. Of the 55 percent of sample agreements specifying the amount of time allowed, 66 percent grant half-hour lunch periods and 20 percent provide an hour.

Nineteen percent of contracts provide paid lunch periods; two-thirds of these pay only under certain conditions.

Provisions for working through the regular lunch period are found in 22 percent of the sample. Twenty-six percent of these clauses call for regular pay. Of the 16 percent of contracts that provide overtime pay, 34 percent grant overtime pay only after a certain number of hours without lunch.

Lunch-Time Provisions

(Frequency Expressed as Percentage of Contracts*)

	Lunch Time	Amount of Time	Less than 30 mins.	30 mins.	31-59 mins.	One Hour
All Industries	65	55	7	36	*	11
Manufacturing	56	46	9	31	*	6
Non-manufacturing	79	68	4	45	1	18

* Less than 1 percent

Meals during overtime hours are mentioned in 32 percent of agreements surveyed. Under contracts detailing meal provisions, 30 percent call for a paid lunch period; 29 percent pay a meal allowance; 13 percent provide the option of an allowance or a meal furnished by the company; 12 percent call for a company-furnished meal; and 10 percent provide for a paid lunch period and a meal furnished by the company.

Six percent of clauses dealing with overtime meals restrict this provision to employees who are not given advance notice of overtime.

Usually an overtime meal or allowance is called for only after a specified number of hours of overtime (although a few contracts specify work to a certain hour); this is true in 30 percent of agreements in the database. While overtime requirements range from one hour to nine hours, the most common requirements found in contracts containing such provisions are two hours (62 percent), three hours (11 percent), and four hours (8 percent). Forty percent of contracts dealing with overtime meal requirements call for a second meal or allowance after an additional period of overtime work. Of these, 53 percent require four hours of overtime; 26 percent require five hours; and 9 percent require six hours.

Industry pattern: Clauses concerning overtime meals appear in 27 percent of manufacturing contracts and in 40 percent of non-manufacturing contracts. All petroleum, 90 percent of utilities, 83 percent of mining, and 81 percent of chemical industry agreements contain this provision. At least one-third of contracts in communications, construction, foods, maritime, paper, primary metals, and transportation contain overtime meal provisions.

Rest periods are referred to in 44 percent of agreements analyzed. Of these, 9 percent merely state that rest periods will be allowed according to plant or past practice, and 26 percent provide additional breaks during overtime hours. Under contracts containing details on rest periods, 87 percent provide two breaks per shift. Of agreements specifying the amount of time allowed, 56 percent provide 10-minute breaks, and 35 percent provide 15-minute breaks.

Industry pattern: Rest periods are referred to in 42 percent of manufacturing agreements and in 47 percent of non-manufacturing agreements. Such provisions are found in one-half or more of communications, fabricated metals, foods, furniture, insurance and finance, leather, maritime, retail, and services contracts.

Time to clean up and prepare for or cease work is considered in 22 percent of contracts—25 percent in manufacturing and 16 percent in non-manufacturing. Of contracts containing such provisions, 58 percent provide for personal washup time and 12 percent for clothes-changing time. Thirty-seven percent of the provisions grant time for returning tools, checking equipment, or filing required reports. Of clauses stating the amount of time allowed, 43 percent specify ten minutes, and 38 percent specify 5 minutes.

Industry pattern: Provisions concerning time to clean up and prepare for or cease work are most common in furniture and chemicals (each 50 percent), and petroleum (43 percent) agreements.

Other Non-productive Time

Payment for time lost on a day of injury is provided for in 45 percent of the sample contracts. This provision appears in 54 percent of manufacturing and 32 percent of non-manufacturing contracts. Typical clauses state that an employee leaving work because of an injury shall receive a full day's pay, regardless of the time of the injury. All rubber and more than 50 percent of fabricated metals, foods, machinery, mining, primary metals, printing, retail, and transportation equipment contracts provide pay for time lost on the day of injury.

Waiting time —time spent while waiting for work or materials—is considered in 16 percent of the sample (16 percent in manufacturing and 17 percent in non-manufacturing). Of these provisions, 91 percent provide full pay for waiting time; the remainder provide less than full pay. Waiting time provisions appear most frequently in rubber (67 percent) and leather (50 percent) contracts.

Standby time (time spent at home but on call) provisions are found in 4 percent of the sample, appearing in 1 percent of manufacturing agreements and 7 percent of non-manufacturing agreements. Fifty percent of these provisions call for full pay; 50 percent for less than full pay.

Travel time pay of one type or another is provided in 21 percent of agreements. Such provisions appear in a greater proportion of contracts in non-manufacturing industries (41 percent) than in manufacturing (9 percent). Although there is some overlapping in types of paid travel time, usually they fall into one or more of the following categories: portal-to-portal; when called in to work outside of regular work hours; when traveling outside a specified area; and when traveling away from a home office or headquarters. Such provisions are found in all communications and in 60 percent or more of maritime, transportation, and utilities contracts; the rest are scattered throughout the sample.

Voting time (required by law in many states) is mentioned in 6 percent of agreements. Of these, 67 percent provide time off with pay, 17 percent call for time off without pay, and 17 percent state that time off will be given as required by state law.

Negotiating time pay (including a requirement that negotiations be held during work hours) is included in 10 percent of the agreements studied—13 percent in manufacturing and 4 percent in non-manufacturing agreements.

————————

8

Holidays

Holidays are provided in 99 percent of contracts comprising the basic patterns database sample. All or some of these holidays are observed without loss of pay in 90 percent of agreements.

Geographic analysis of the database shows that contracts calling for a bare bones schedule of seven and one-half or fewer holidays are concentrated in the Rocky Mountain region (40 percent); contracts calling for an ample schedule of 12 or more holidays predominate in the Middle Atlantic and North Central regions (each 39 percent).

Ten or more holidays are found in just under three-quarters of agreements, having risen in frequency from 7 percent in 1966 to 72 percent in the present survey. The number of contracts providing 12 or more holidays also has risen sharply, climbing from 3 percent in 1971 to 31 percent in this study. Fourteen or more holidays are called for in 8 percent of agreements analyzed.

Number of Holidays

The median number of holidays provided in the total sample is 11, the same as in the previous study. Two contracts with holiday provisions provide only five holidays (the lowest number in the sample), while another two contracts call for 19 (the highest).

Number of Holidays Provided

(Frequency Expressed as Percentage of Provisions)

	Fewer than 8	8-8½	9-9½	10-10½	11-11½	12-12½	13-13½	14 or more
All Industries	9	7	11	21	21	15	8	8
Manufacturing	2	4	7	22	25	17	13	10
Non-manufacturing	21	11	17	18	14	11	1	5

In non-manufacturing the median number of holidays is 9 and in manufacturing the median is 11. Ten or more holidays are provided in 87 percent of manufacturing agreements, compared with 50 percent of non-manufacturing agreements. Fewer than 10 holidays are found in one-half of non-manufacturing contracts and in only 13 percent of manufacturing agreements.

Trend in Number of Holidays

(Frequency Expressed as Percentage of Contracts)

	1961	1966	1971	1975	1979	1983	1986	1989	1992
None specified	1	1	1	1	2	2	2	1	2
Fewer than 7	22	16	11	6	4	3	3	5	5
7-7½	47	39	15	10	8	5	6	4	5
8-8½	23	31	25	12	11	8	8	8	7
9-9½	5	7	27	29	17	11	9	11	11
10-10½	5[1]	7[1]	16	20	27	23	23	18	21
11-11½	—	—	4	12	15	20	18	22	21
12-12½	—	—	3[2]	10[2]	11	13	14	14	15
13-13½	—	—	—	—	6[3]	7	10	8	8
14 or more	—	—	—	—	—	9	9	9	8

[1] 10 or more.
[2] 12 or more.
[3] 13 or more.

Industry pattern: All manufacturing contracts in the sample provide some holidays. In non-manufacturing, 96 percent of agreements contain a holiday clause, the exceptions being five contracts in transportation and one in insurance and finance. In addition, one contract in services does not state which holidays are observed.

In eight of the 26 industries studied—chemicals, communications, fabricated metals, foods, insurance and finance, primary metals, rubber, and stone-clay-glass—the median number of holidays is 11. The median is 10 in furniture, leather, lumber, mining, petroleum, printing, and transportation. The lowest median is seven in construction; the highest is 13 in transportation equipment.

In the remaining industries, medians are 9 in retail, services, and textiles; 10.5 in utilities; 11.25 in electrical machinery; 12 in apparel, machinery, and paper; and 12.75 in maritime.

Number of Holidays, By Region

(Frequency Expressed as Percentage of Contracts in Each Region*)

	Fewer than 7	7-7½	8-8½	9-9½	10-10½	11-11½	12-12½	13-13½	14 or more
Middle Atlantic	5	4	4	9	18	22	20	11	9
Midwest	7	11	4	11	21	25	11	7	4
Northeast	—	4	4	12	12	31	19	12	8
North Central	4	3	2	8	19	25	16	10	13
Rocky Mountain	30	10	10	10	20	20	—	—	—
Southeast	4	9	9	17	26	13	11	13	—
Southwest	—	8	8	23	15	31	8	8	—
West Coast	—	4	29	16	16	16	11	—	7
Multiregion	6	2	—	6	33	12	15	4	13

*See p. xi for area designations.

Days Observed as Holidays

Christmas Day is observed in all but four contracts specifying holidays, Labor Day and Thanksgiving each are found in all but six, New Year's Day in all but nine, Independence Day in all but 10, and Memorial Day in all but 16. These six traditional holidays appear as a group in 92 percent of sample contracts.

Following in frequency are three holidays found in at least one-half of agreements analyzed: the day after Thanksgiving (60 percent), a full day on Christmas Eve (53 percent), and part or all of Good Friday (50 percent).

New Year's Eve appears as a full holiday in 32 percent of sample contracts, as does Washington's Birthday. Twenty percent observe an employee's birthday as a holiday, and 16 percent each recognize Veterans Day, floating holidays, and personal days.

The frequency of sample agreements listing Martin Luther King's Birthday as a holiday remains at 14 percent, after rising 5 percentage points from 1986 to 1989. Regionally, Martin Luther King's Birthday appears most frequently in West Coast, Middle Atlantic states, and multiregion contracts, and least often in the Rocky Mountain, Southeast, and Southwest regions.

Other less celebrated holidays found in the sample include a full Christmas-New Year's week (13 percent); Columbus Day (9 percent); selected days between Christmas and New Year's (8 percent); Election Day (7 percent); one or more days chosen locally (5 percent); Easter Monday (4 percent); Lincoln's Birthday (3 percent); and the eves of Christmas and New Year's as half holidays (2 percent and 1 percent, respectively).

Holidays other than those listed above are found in 28 percent of the 400 contracts. Among these are the day before or after another holiday to provide a long weekend, Easter Sunday, a "bonus" day, an employee's anniversary date of employment, Yom Kippur, Rosh Hashanah, Flag Day, Inauguration Day, May Day, and days of local or regional significance such as Patriot's Day, Mardi Gras, Pioneer Day, and the first day of deer season. In 14 percent of contracts, days observed vary from year to year.

Industry pattern: Extra time off during the Christmas season and days such as the Friday after Thanksgiving to stretch a holiday into a long weekend are found more often in manufacturing contracts than in non-manufacturing. Days observed on varying dates from year to year also are more prevalent in manufacturing.

In non-manufacturing industries, on the other hand, extra time to create long weekends is avoided, and holidays such as Washington's Birthday, Veterans Day, Columbus Day, and Lincoln's Birthday are more common. Individualized holidays such as personal time and employee birthdays also prevail in non-manufacturing.

Most Commonly Observed Holidays

(Frequency Expressed as Percentage of Contracts)

Holiday	All Industries	Manu-facturing	Non-manu-facturing
Christmas	98	99	95
Labor Day	97	99	94
Thanksgiving	97	98	95
Independence Day	96	97	94
New Year's Day	96	98	94
Memorial Day	95	96	92
Day after Thanksgiving	60	80	27
Christmas Eve, full day	53	73	20
Good Friday, including ½ day	50	70	19
New Year's Eve, full day	32	47	8
Washington's Birthday	32	27	39
Employee's birthday	20	15	27
Floating day	16	17	15
Personal day	16	10	25
Veterans Day	16	11	25
Martin Luther King's Birthday	14	9	22
Christmas-New Year's week	13	20	—
Columbus Day	9	7	12
Other days during Christmas week	8	12	1
Election Day	7	7	6
Day chosen locally	5	5	5
Easter Monday	4	6	2
Lincoln's Birthday	3	1	5
Christmas Eve, ½ day	2	1	3
New Year's Eve, ½ day	1	1	1

The traditional six holidays are provided in 94 percent of manufacturing and in 90 percent of non-manufacturing contracts. Good Friday as a full or half holiday is far more common in manufacturing (70 percent) than non-manufacturing (19 percent). It is found in three-quarters or more of agreements in apparel, chemicals, electrical machinery, fabricated metals, furniture, leather, machinery, petroleum, and primary metals. Utilities is the only non-manufacturing industry in which a majority of contracts provide Good Friday as a holiday.

The day after Thanksgiving is called for in 80 percent of manufacturing agreements and in 27 percent of non-manufacturing contracts. Manufacturing industries in which three-quarters or more of contracts provide the day after Thanksgiving as a holiday are apparel, chemicals, electrical machinery, fabricated metals, furniture, leather, lumber, machinery, petroleum, primary metals, stone-clay-glass, and transportation equipment. In non-manufacturing the day after Thanksgiving is listed as a holiday in at least one-half of communications, insurance and finance, and utilities agreements.

Christmas Eve is observed as a full day in 73 percent of manufacturing agreements and as a half day in 1 percent, compared with 20 percent as a full day and 3 percent as a half day in non-manufacturing agreements. Full or partial observance of Christmas Eve is called for in more than four-fifths of contracts in electrical machinery, fabricated metals, furniture, lumber, machinery, paper, primary metals, and transportation equipment. Mining and utilities are the only non-manufacturing industries in which more than half of the contracts provide Christmas Eve as a holiday.

New Year's Eve is a full or half holiday in 48 percent of manufacturing contracts, compared with only 10 percent of non-manufacturing agreements. At least two-thirds of contracts in fabricated metals, machinery, rubber, and transportation equipment call for this holiday. Observance of the entire Christmas-to-New Year's week is found only in manufacturing. The full week is provided in nearly three-quarters of transportation equipment contracts and in three-eighths of machinery agreements.

Washington's Birthday is more common in non-manufacturing (39 percent) than manufacturing (27 percent). At least one-half of sample agreements in apparel, communications, foods, insurance and finance, maritime, petroleum, and utilities provide time off on this holiday.

An employee's birthday, observed in 15 percent of manufacturing contracts and 27 percent of non-manufacturing contracts, is found in at least one-half of printing, retail, rubber, and transportation agreements. Floating holidays, which appear in 17 percent of manufacturing contracts and 15 percent of non-manufacturing agreements, are provided for in from one-quarter to one-half of agreements in chemicals, communications, furniture, leather, lumber, paper, petroleum, and services.

Veterans Day is observed in 11 percent of the manufacturing and in 25 percent of the non-manufacturing sample. One-quarter or more of contracts in foods, insurance and finance, leather, maritime, stone-clay-glass, and utilities provide Veterans Day as a holiday.

Occurring with almost the same frequency as Veterans Day are personal holidays (10 percent of manufacturing and 25 percent of non-manufacturing agreements). Personal days are observed in 63 percent of retail, 44 percent of apparel, 40 percent of communications, and 25 percent to 30 percent of chemicals, insurance and finance, leather, mining, printing, and services industries agreements.

Columbus Day appears in 7 percent of manufacturing contracts and in 12 percent of non-manufacturing agreements. Observance of this holiday is most prevalent in contracts in: maritime (63 percent), apparel (56 percent), and insurance and finance (29 percent).

Most Common Holidays by Industry

(Frequency Expressed as Percentage of Industry Contracts)

	New Year's Day	Washington's Birthday	Good Friday (full or 1/2 day)	Memorial Day	Independence Day	Labor Day	Veterans Day	Thanksgiving Day	Day After Thanksgiving	Christmas Eve (full or 1/2 day)	Christmas Day	New Year's Eve (full or 1/2 day)	Employee's birthday	Floating day
ALL INDUSTRIES	96	32	50	95	96	97	16	97	60	54	98	33	20	16
MANUFACTURING	98	27	70	96	97	99	11	98	80	74	99	48	15	17
Apparel	89	89	100	100	89	100	—	100	89	22	100	22	22	—
Chemicals	100	31	88	100	100	100	19	100	88	69	100	31	13	44
Electrical Machinery	100	45	80	100	100	100	10	100	80	90	100	45	—	10
Fabricated Metals	100	5	79	89	95	100	16	100	95	89	100	68	26	21
Foods	100	67	48	100	100	100	33	100	48	38	100	29	29	5
Furniture	100	—	83	100	100	100	17	100	100	83	100	50	17	33
Leather	75	25	75	100	50	100	25	100	100	75	75	—	—	25
Lumber	100	14	57	100	100	100	—	100	86	100	100	43	43	29
Machinery	100	12	81	100	100	100	4	100	100	88	100	73	8	15
Paper	79	—	43	79	86	86	7	79	43	86	93	21	36	43
Petroleum	100	57	100	100	100	100	14	100	100	29	100	—	—	29
Primary Metals	100	32	92	100	100	100	4	96	84	88	100	48	—	8
Printing	100	38	25	100	100	100	13	100	38	50	100	38	50	13
Rubber	100	17	33	100	100	100	—	100	67	50	100	67	50	—
Stone, Clay & Glass	92	23	62	92	100	100	38	100	77	69	100	8	23	15
Textiles	100	10	40	70	100	100	—	100	30	60	100	10	10	20
Transportation Equipment	100	9	65	97	97	100	—	100	100	85	100	97	—	12
NON-MANUFACTURING	94	39	19	92	94	94	25	95	27	23	95	10	27	15
Communications	100	50	30	90	90	90	20	100	50	20	100	20	20	50
Construction	100	24	7	100	100	97	21	100	34	3	100	3	—	—
Insurance & Finance	86	57	43	86	86	86	29	86	57	43	86	14	14	14
Maritime	100	100	38	100	100	100	100	100	—	38	100	25	—	—
Mining	92	8	33	92	92	100	8	92	42	75	92	17	17	—
Retail	100	37	—	93	100	96	22	100	7	22	100	7	52	4
Services	93	44	11	93	96	96	—	96	7	7	96	7	33	30
Transportation	80	32	24	80	80	80	20	80	28	16	80	4	52	24
Utilities	100	60	60	100	100	100	80	100	70	60	100	20	10	20

Holiday Pay _____

Holiday pay is discussed in 91 percent of sample agreements—in all but one manufacturing contract and in percent of non-manufacturing agreements. All recognized holidays are paid in 96 percent of contracts with holiday pay provisions—97 percent in manufacturing and 95 percent in non-manufacturing. Three percent provide for some paid and some unpaid holidays. Only two agreements, both in construction, state that no pay will be provided for holidays.

Holiday Pay Provisions

(Frequency Expressed as Percentage of Provisions)

	Holidays Provided[1]	All Named Holidays Paid	Some Named Holidays Paid
All Industries	99	96	3
Manufacturing	100	97	3
Non-manufacturing	96	95	3

[1]Based on all sample contracts.

Eligibility for Holiday Pay _____

Eligibility requirements for holiday pay generally are of two types: a length-of-service requirement and a work requirement. At least one of these two requirements is found in 88 percent of contracts with holiday pay provisions; in many cases both appear. Eligibility requirements are found in 95 percent of manufacturing holiday pay provisions and 75 percent of non-manufacturing provisions.

Length-of-service requirements are stipulated in 54 percent of holiday pay provisions. Four weeks is the most common requirement, found in 39 percent of clauses containing such prerequisites. Three months of service is required under 21 percent of length-of-service requirements, two months under 20 percent, six weeks under 7 percent, and six months under 6 percent. Two length-of-service requirements are for less than four weeks, while six range from 15 weeks to 24 weeks of service. The service period required often is equal to the length of the probationary period.

Work requirements appear in 85 percent of holiday pay provisions. In nearly four-fifths of work requirement provisions, an employee must work the day before and the day after a holiday to receive holiday pay. Nine percent of such clauses call for work at some time during the week, 3 percent require work only on the day before or after a holiday, and 9 percent specify some other requirement, generally more liberal. Under 93 percent of these provisions, work requirements may be waived for excused absences or lay-offs.

In addition, an employee who fails to report for scheduled holiday work is denied holiday pay under 40 percent of sample contracts.

Industry pattern: Length-of-service requirements appear in 60 percent of holiday pay provisions in manufacturing industry contracts and in 41 percent of those in non-manufacturing. Work requirements are specified in 91 percent of manufacturing and in 72 percent of non-manufacturing holiday pay clauses. Showing up for scheduled holiday work is a pay requirement in 51 percent of manufacturing and 21 percent of non-manufacturing contracts.

Length-of-service requirements appear in all holiday pay provisions in furniture and leather, and in two-thirds or more of provisions in electrical machinery, lumber, mining, paper, primary metals, stone-clay-glass, textiles, and transportation equipment. Work requirements are found in every holiday pay clause in apparel, leather, lumber, maritime, rubber, and stone-clay-glass, and in at least three-fourths of provisions in chemicals, electrical machinery, fabricated metals, foods, furniture, machinery, mining, paper, petroleum, primary metals, retail, textiles, and transportation equipment.

Provisions calling for waiver of work requirements appear in all contracts in leather, lumber, rubber, and stone-clay-glass, and in at least one-half of agreements in all other industries, except construction, insurance and finance, maritime, printing, and utilities.

Failure to report for holiday work is penalized in all petroleum and rubber contracts, and in at least one-half of agreements in chemicals, fabricated metals, mining, paper, primary metals, stone-clay-glass, and transportation equipment. No such provisions are found in the following industries: apparel, construction, insurance and finance, leather, maritime, printing, and utilities.

Holidays Falling on Scheduled Time Off

Provision for a holiday occurring on Saturday is found in 42 percent of the total sample. In 80 percent of these clauses an alternate day off is granted, while only pay is provided in 19 percent. Saturday holiday clauses appear in 52 percent of manufacturing contracts and in 25 percent of non-manufacturing contracts.

Holidays falling on Sunday are referred to in 68 percent of agreements analyzed—74 percent in manufacturing and 59 percent in non-manufacturing. An alternate day off is arranged in 98 percent of these provisions.

In addition to contracts that specify arrangements for holidays falling on Saturday or Sunday, a number of contracts contain general provisions stating that all holidays will be celebrated regardless of the day on which they fall or that holidays will be celebrated on days observed by the federal or state government. Further, some agreements list specific dates on which holidays are to be observed during the life of the agreement.

Provision for a holiday occurring on an employee's day off is found in 19 percent of the sample, and such clauses are more prevalent in non-manufacturing (27 percent) than in manufacturing (14 percent). Alternate day-off clauses prevail in non-manufacturing agreements (63 percent); pay-only clauses prevail in manufacturing agreements (67 percent).

Holidays falling during an employee's vacation are discussed in 71 percent of contracts studied. Of these provisions, 44 percent provide pay only, 31 percent call for an additional day off, and 26 percent permit either an extra day's pay or an extra day off. Of clauses providing an option, more than three-eighths leave the choice to employees. Holidays during a vacation are more often found in manufacturing (78 percent) than in non-manufacturing (61 percent). Pay only is called for in 52 percent of manufacturing agreements; an alternate day off is provided in 38 percent of non-manufacturing contracts.

Pay for Holidays Worked

Compensation for holiday work is provided in 94 percent of sample contracts. Such pay is expressed as holiday pay plus pay for hours actually worked in 65 percent of these provisions and as pay only for hours worked in 30 percent. Five percent of contracts addressing the issue provide some other type of compensation such as a different rate of pay for work on different holidays.

Under contracts discussing compensation for work on a holiday, the most common payments are holiday pay plus doubletime and holiday pay plus time and one-half (each 29 percent). Following in frequency are pay only for hours worked at doubletime (13 percent) and pay only for hours worked at doubletime and one-half (10 percent).

A higher premium after a certain number of hours worked on a holiday is specified in 11 percent of pay for holiday work provisions. In almost all cases the higher premium is applied to hours after a full shift has been worked or to hours outside the normal schedule.

Rate of Pay for Holiday Work

(Frequency Expressed as Percentage of Holiday Work Provisions)

	Holiday Pay Plus Pay for Hours Worked at:			Pay Only for Hours Worked at:			
	1	1½	2	1½	2	2½	3
All Industries	4	29	29	2	13	10	4
Manufacturing	3	30	39	1	6	11	5
Non-manufacturing	6	29	11	4	26	9	3

Industry pattern: Premium pay for holiday work generally is higher in manufacturing agreements than in non-manufacturing contracts. The highest premiums (tripletime for hours worked or holiday pay plus doubletime) predominate in electrical machinery, fabricated metals, furniture, machinery, rubber, and transportation equipment, and are found frequently in chemicals, foods, primary metals, printing, and retail. The lowest premiums (holiday pay plus straight-time or doubletime for hours worked) predominate in construction and printing, and appear frequently in transportation and services.

Limitations Upon Management

Restrictions on management's right to schedule work on holidays are found in 27 percent of the sample. Nearly three-quarters of these clauses place a limited prohibition on holiday work; almost one-quarter require advance notice. Only five contracts in the sample flatly forbid work on holidays.

A minimum work or pay guarantee is applied specifically to holiday work in 17 percent of the sample. In 49 percent of these provisions four hours must be paid or provided. Eight hours is the minimum specified in 31 percent of the clauses and two hours is the minimum in 8 percent. The guaranteed minimum is paid at higher than straight-time in 52 percent of the provisions.

Industry pattern: Restrictions on holiday work are found more frequently in non-manufacturing (34 percent) than in manufacturing (22 percent). Restrictions are most prevalent in agreements in furniture (67 percent); construction (59 percent); and maritime, rubber, and utilities (each 50 percent). These also appear in one-third to one-half of agreements in apparel, lumber, and retail; and in one-quarter to one-third of contracts in insurance and finance, leather, machinery, paper, printing, and transportation equipment.

Minimum work or pay guarantees also are more common in non-manufacturing contracts (27 percent) than in manufacturing agreements (11 percent). A minimum guarantee is found in 63 percent of printing contracts; one-third to one-half of contracts in communications, maritime, and rubber; and one-quarter to one-third of contracts in insurance and finance, transportation, and utilities.

9

Layoff, Rehiring, and Work Sharing

Layoff provisions are included in 94 percent of the Basic Patterns database. Seniority is a factor in selecting employees for layoff in 88 percent of the contracts—96 percent in manufacturing and 74 percent in non-manufacturing.

Geographic analysis of the sample contracts indicates that layoff provisions are prevalent in all regions designated in the database, ranging from 89 percent in each the multiregion, Northeast, and West Coast areas to 100 percent in the Midwest and Southeast.

Seniority is the sole consideration in selecting employees to be laid off in 47 percent of sample contracts.

Seniority is the determining factor in layoffs under 27 percent of the agreements included in the study. These provisions call for retention of more senior employees during a reduction in force only if they are qualified for available jobs.

Seniority is a secondary factor, to be considered only when factors such as ability and physical fitness are equal, in 14 percent of the contracts.

Industry pattern: Seniority is the sole or determining factor in at least two-thirds each of manufacturing industry contracts and non-manufacturing industry contracts except those in construction, maritime, and mining.

Consideration of Seniority in Layoff

(Frequency Expressed as Percentage of Contracts)

	Applied in Some Degree	Sole Factor	Determining Factor	Secondary Factor
All Industries	88	47	27	14
Manufacturing	96	48	33	16
Non-manufacturing	74	44	19	11

Exceptions from Seniority Rules in Layoffs

Exceptions from seniority in layoffs are allowed in 49 percent of the sample contracts, and more than three-fourths of these provisions give union representatives superseniority for layoff purposes. Under superseniority provisions, union stewards and local officials are the last employees to be laid off. Of contracts granting union representatives superseniority, 48 percent stipulate that the representatives must be qualified for available jobs to be exempt from layoff provisions.

Industry pattern: Union representatives are given top seniority for layoff purposes in at least one-half the contracts in the following industries: electrical machinery, fabricated metals, furniture, machinery, primary metals, textiles, and transportation equipment.

Specially skilled employees, whose employment is necessary for continuous and efficient company operations, are exempt from layoff provisions in 25 percent of procedures containing seniority exceptions.

Seniority rules may be waived during temporary (usually less than two weeks) or emergency layoffs in 29 percent of contracts specifying exceptions to layoff procedures—32 percent in manufacturing and 20 percent in non-manufacturing.

Seniority employees may elect layoff out of order in 15 percent of sample contracts—20 percent in manufacturing and 7 percent in non-manufacturing.

Notice of Layoff

Advance notice by the company of impending layoff to the affected employee, the union, or both, is required in 50 percent of sample agreements—57 percent of manufacturing contracts and 38 percent of non-manufacturing contracts.

Of agreements requiring advance notice of layoffs, 36 percent specify notification to the employee; 23 percent specify notification to the union; 40 percent specify notification to both.

Advance Notice to Employees

(Frequency Expressed as Percentage of Notice Provisions)

	No Minimum	1 or 2 Days	3 or 4 Days	5 Days	7 or More Days
All Industries	14	16	16	14	18
Manufacturing	11	23	20	12	9
Non-manufacturing	20	—	5	19	39

Advance Notice to Unions

(Frequency Expressed as Percentage of Notice Provisions)

	No Minimum	1 or 2 Days	3 or 4 Days	5 Days	7 or More Days
All Industries	18	14	10	8	14
Manufacturing	14	19	14	9	12
Non-manufacturing	25	3	—	7	19

Under agreements specifying amount of advance layoff notice to employees, 50 percent stipulate one to four days' notice; 50 percent stipulate five days or more. In contracts specifying amount of notice to the union, 52 percent require one to four days' notice; 48 percent require five or more days.

Industry pattern: Notice-of-layoff provisions are found in at least two-thirds of contracts in chemicals, communications, electrical machinery, fabricated metals, furniture, machinery, rubber, and transportation equipment industries.

Bumping

Employees scheduled for layoff are permitted to displace less senior workers in other jobs under 61 percent of agreements included in the survey—75 percent in manufacturing and 40 percent in non-manufacturing.

Of bumping rights clauses, 71 percent state that employees must be qualified to perform the job they desire to bump into. Service requirements ranging from one to 16 years are specified in 6 percent of bumping provisions, and break-in periods for employees to demonstrate their qualifications for the job are called for in 25 percent.

Bumping throughout the company is permitted in 8 percent of contracts specifying the permissible bumping area; bumping throughout the plant in 21 percent. Bumping is restricted to a division or department in 17 percent of these clauses, while in 48 percent bumping is restricted to an employee's classification or group. Four percent of the provisions allow employees to bump only to their former job, classification, or group.

Of the 92 percent of bumping provisions specifying who may be displaced, 53 percent specify the least senior employee, and 45 percent specify any less senior employee.

Industry pattern: Bumping is allowed in at least three-quarters of contracts in the following industries: chemicals, electrical machinery, fabricated metals, furniture, leather, machinery, mining, primary metals, rubber, and textiles. More than 60 percent of electrical machinery, fabricated metals, furniture, leather, machinery, paper, rubber, and textiles industry agreements specify that an employee desiring to exercise bumping rights must be qualified to perform the job.

Recall

Recall of employees after layoff is provided for in 86 percent of contracts in the database. Of these provisions, 41 percent recall employees in reverse order of layoff, and 50 percent recall employees in reverse order of layoff only if they are qualified to perform available jobs. Laid-off employees have preference over new hires in 35 percent of contracts containing recall provisions.

Work Sharing

Clauses providing for work sharing as an alternative or prelude to layoffs are included in 17 percent of the sample—23 percent in manufacturing and 7 percent in non-manufacturing. Of contracts providing for work sharing, 41 percent specify that work sharing may be implemented for a limited time, and 38 percent state that the company must consult with the union before work sharing may be implemented.

Layoff Provisions

(Frequency Expressed as Percentage of Industry Contracts)

	Seniority Applied in Layoffs	Exceptions From Seniority allowed	Advance Notice of Layoff Required	Recall After Layoff Specified	Bumping Permitted	Worksharing Provided
ALL INDUSTRIES	88	49	50	86	61	17
MANUFACTURING	96	62	57	96	75	23
Apparel	67	—	—	89	—	78
Chemicals	100	69	69	94	75	6
Electrical Machinery	100	95	90	100	95	30
Fabricated Metals	100	79	74	95	89	26
Foods	100	29	43	95	67	5
Furniture	100	100	83	100	83	33
Leather	100	25	25	100	100	25
Lumber	100	43	29	100	57	—
Machinery	100	81	73	100	96	42
Paper	93	36	43	93	71	7
Petroleum	100	14	43	86	57	—
Primary Metals	96	68	56	100	84	24
Printing	100	25	50	75	38	13
Rubber	83	50	83	100	83	33
Stone-Clay-Glass	100	31	23	100	62	31
Textiles	100	80	20	90	80	20
Transportation Equipment	91	88	68	97	71	21
NON-MANUFACTURING	74	29	38	70	40	7
Communications	100	30	100	100	70	30
Construction	3	38	28	3	—	3
Insurance & Finance	71	43	29	71	57	—
Maritime	50	—	—	50	—	—
Mining	83	58	42	83	92	8
Retail	96	44	33	96	33	11
Services	93	26	37	85	44	7
Transportation	96	8	52	84	64	—
Utilities	90	—	20	80	30	10

10

Leave of Absence

Leave of absence provisions appear in 92 percent of the 400 sample contracts contained in CBNC's database, the same percentage as in the 1989 and 1986 Basic Patterns studies. Geographic analysis shows that from 70 to 96 percent of contracts in regions designated in the database contain leave provisions.

Some form of leave of absence is provided for in all but one manufacturing agreement and in all but four non-manufacturing contracts outside the construction industry; only one construction contract includes a leave of absence provision. Eight major types of leave are included in the study—personal, union business, military, family, civic duty, funeral, unpaid sick leave, and paid sick leave.

Leave of Absence Provisions

(Frequency Expressed as Percentage of Contracts)

	Per-sonal	Union	Fam-ily	Fu-neral	Civic	Paid Sick	Unpaid Sick	Mili-tary
All Industries	76	76	35	85	82	32	53	71
Manufacturing	86	86	38	96	94	23	55	81
Non-manufacturing	61	60	29	68	63	47	49	56

Personal Leave

Leave of absence for personal or unspecified reasons is provided in 76 percent of agreements included in the database. Some contracts simply state that personal leave will be granted for "good" or "sufficient" reason, subject to the approval of the employer, while others specify reasons such as family illness or personal business.

Duration of leave is mentioned in 81 percent of the contracts allowing personal leave and ranges from one week to one year. Of agreements that discuss duration, 33 percent allow an initial one-month leave period, 21 percent allow three months, and 13 percent specify a "reasonable" or unspecified period. Extension of the initial leave period is allowed in 50 percent of personal leave provisions analyzed.

Effect on seniority is discussed in 73 percent of personal leave provisions. Of the seniority clauses, 40 percent provide for retention during leave, 55 percent provide for accumulation for the length of leave, and 5 percent provide for accumulation for a specified period and then retention. A time limit is imposed on retention and/or accumulation in 22 percent of the clauses that discuss seniority. It should be noted, however, that contract language on seniority often is ambiguous. *

---

* For purposes of tabulation, clauses stating that "there shall be no loss of seniority during leave" have been considered as providing for retention—without accumulation—of seniority. This method has been followed throughout this section.

Early return from personal leave is specifically allowed in 7 percent of personal leave clauses; advance notice of an employee's intent to return to work is required in 9 percent.

Reemployment rights are discussed in 33 percent of personal leave clauses. Of agreements containing reemployment rights provisions, 43 percent guarantee employees their former job or an equivalent, 20 percent guarantee the former job or an equivalent if it is not held by a more senior employee, and 21 percent provide a "general right" to reemployment.

Violation of leave conditions is discussed in 77 percent of personal leave clauses. Failure to return on time is the most frequently mentioned leave violation, cited in 43 percent of clauses dealing with the subject; failure to return on time except in an emergency or with company approval is cited in 28 percent. Thirty-six percent of violation clauses refer to working elsewhere; 30 percent cite working elsewhere without company approval. Sixteen percent of these clauses cite falsifying an application for leave as a violation. Many contracts specify more than one type of leave violation.

Discharge is a penalty for leave violations in 61 percent of contracts discussing violations; 59 percent impose loss of seniority as a penalty. Both penalties are included in some agreements.

Approval of personal leave is a management prerogative in 56 percent of contracts containing personal leave provisions, while both management and union approval is required in 13 percent. Twenty-six percent of personal leave clauses call for management approval with notice to the union.

Industry pattern: Personal leave provisions appear in 86 percent of manufacturing contracts and 61 percent (or 75 percent excluding construction) of non-manufacturing agreements. Personal leave is provided for in all furniture, rubber, and leather industry contracts, and in all but one each of communications, lumber, fabricated metals, paper, transportation equipment, petroleum, and apparel agreements. Insurance and finance and construction are the only industries in which less than one-half of contracts call for personal leave.

Union Leave

Leave to perform union duties is found in 76 percent of contracts in the database—86 percent in manufacturing and 60 percent in non-manufacturing.

Long-term leave to assume union office or to participate in other union business is provided in 70 percent of the contracts analyzed. These provisions are found in 81 percent of manufacturing agreements and in 52 percent of non-manufacturing contracts. More than one-third (38 percent) of long-term leave provisions limit the number of employees who may be granted leave at the same time.

Duration of long-term leave is specified in 91 percent of contracts providing such leave. Leave for a one-year period and for term of office each are specified in 34 percent of clauses specifying duration. In 8 percent of these provisions leave for a three-year period is allowed. Extension of the initial leave period is allowed in 45 percent of long-term leave provisions.

Effect on seniority is discussed in 89 percent of long-term union leave provisions. Seniority accumulates for the length of leave in 64 percent of the seniority provisions and is retained in 34 percent. Only 2 percent of these clauses provide for accumulation for a specified period followed by retention.

Short-term leave to attend union conventions and conferences is allowed in 49 percent of contracts in the database and is more common in manufacturing agreements (54 percent) than in non-manufacturing agreements (41 percent). The number of employees permitted to take short-term leave at one time is restricted in 51 percent of such clauses.

Industry pattern: All contracts in rubber, textiles, fabricated metals, communications, paper, petroleum, furniture, and leather industries provide for union leave. Such provisions are included in half or more of contracts in 14 other industries. Only in printing, apparel, maritime, and construction industries do less than one-half of agreements contain union leave provisions.

Union Leave Provisions

(Frequency Expressed as Number of Contracts)

	Long-Term Leave							Short-Term Leave	
			Length of Leave Permitted				No. of employees on leave limited	No. of provisions	No. of employees on leave limited
	No. of provisions	Term of Office	Term of Contract	Less than one year	One year	More than one year			
All Industries	304	87	9	15	87	56	107	196	99
Manufacturing	211	58	6	10	69	39	90	133	71
Non-manufacturing	93	29	3	5	18	17	17	63	28

Family Leave

Family leave provisions are found in 35 percent of sample agreements. All but four of these contracts provide for maternity leave. Parental leave is included in 19 contracts; paternity and adoption leave each in 20. An emerging trend—leave to care for children and/or elderly family members—is reflected in 15 contracts.

Eligibility for family leave is based on length of service under 17 percent of family leave clauses. Three months and one year of service are the most common requirements, appearing each in seven of the 23 contracts containing service requirements. Six contracts require two months of service and three require six months of service.

Effect on seniority is discussed in 73 percent of family leave provisions. Of these, 55 percent allow accumulation of seniority; 41 percent allow retention of seniority. Seniority is accumulated for a specified period of time and then retained in 5 percent of these clauses.

Industry pattern: Family leave is provided in 38 percent of manufacturing agreements and 29 percent of non-manufacturing contracts. Such leave is provided in one-half or more of contracts in rubber, transportation equipment, leather, textiles, electrical machinery, and apparel industries.

Duration of maternity leave is discussed in 76 percent of maternity leave provisions and varies from one month to one year. Under agreements specifying leave duration, the most common periods allowed are six months (41 percent), and one year (16 percent). Leave for three months is granted in 14 percent of such clauses, and 8 percent permit leave for one month. Length of maternity leave is determined by a physician in 23 percent of the contracts that discuss duration. Twenty-four percent of maternity leave provisions require a physical examination or medical certificate upon return to work.

Length of Maternity Leave

(Frequency Expressed as Number of Contracts)

	"Reasonable time"	Set by physician	Maximum Number of Months						
			1	2	3	4	6	9	12
All Industries	4	24	4	1	7	1	20	2	8
Manufacturing	2	20	1	1	5	1	12	1	7
Non-manufacturing	2	4	3	—	2	—	8	1	1

Funeral Leave

Time off for death in an employee's immediate family (as defined by the contract) is granted under 85 percent of sample contracts in the database.

Three days' leave is granted in 83 percent of bereavement clauses; five days' leave in 9 percent; four days' leave in 4 percent. Thirty-eight percent of bereavement clauses grant shorter leaves for death outside the immediate family (as defined by the contract). Of bereavement leave provisions, 40 percent require an employee to attend the funeral, while 24 percent specify that proof of death may be required upon return to work. Only five of the sample contracts charge time spent on bereavement leave against sick or annual leave.

Industry pattern: Funeral leave is more common in manufacturing agreements (96 percent) than in non-manufacturing (68 percent). All contracts in the chemicals, communications, mining, furniture, paper, rubber, leather, petroleum, foods, electrical machinery, lumber, services, and fabricated metals industries provide funeral leave. Insurance and finance, maritime, and construction are the only industries in which less than one-half of the contracts provide funeral leave.

Civic Duty Leave

Leave to perform civic duty appears in 327 of the 400 sample contracts. All but one of these agreements specify leave for jury duty, while 99 grant leave for other court service.

Payment of an employee's regular salary less any jury fees received is provided in 82 percent of jury duty clauses, and payment of full salary regardless of jury fees received is provided in 17 percent. Employees are paid a specified flat amount in 1 percent of jury duty provisions, and another 1 percent are silent on the subject of compensation. Thirty-four percent of jury duty provisions require an employee to work when possible, and 18 percent limit the number of days per year an employee may be paid by the company for jury service.

Leave to assume public office is found in 17 percent of the 400 sample contracts. Duration of such leave usually is limited to one term of office. Six percent of agreements studied allow leave for service in the Peace Corps, and 3 percent allow leave to work in a credit union.

Effect on seniority is discussed in 73 percent of civic duty provisions (other than jury duty or other court service). Of these, 68 percent allow accumulation of seniority and 24 percent provide for retention.

Industry pattern: Civic duty leave appears in 94 percent of manufacturing contracts and in 63 percent of non-manufacturing. At least three-fourths of contracts in foods, furniture, lumber, mining, primary metals, printing, retail, machinery, stone-clay-glass, transportation, and services provide civic duty leave. All contracts in textiles, paper, chemicals, fabricated metals, leather, petroleum, rubber, electrical machinery, transportation equipment, and communications provide civic duty leave.

Paid Sick Leave

Paid sick leave, not sickness and accident insurance (*see section 44*), is provided in 32 percent of the sample contracts.

A length-of-service requirement appears in 74 percent of paid sick leave provisions. One year of service is required in 32 percent of paid leave clauses; six months in 18 percent; and less than six months in 19 percent. A service requirement of more than one year is found in 3 percent of paid sick leave provisions.

Duration is specified in all paid sick leave clauses. Forty-three percent of sick leave clauses grant leave for a flat period of time. Leave is earned on the basis of a specified number of credits per unit of worktime in 30 percent of sick leave provisions. Under 25 percent these clauses, duration varies with an employee's length of service.

Restrictions are placed on accumulation of unused sick leave in 53 percent of sick leave provisions. Pay for at least a portion of unused leave is called for in 48 percent of contracts providing paid sick leave, usually at annual intervals.

Amount of pay granted during sick leave is specified in 93 percent of paid sick leave clauses. Of these, 88 percent provide full pay for the entire period; 7 percent provide partial pay for the entire period; five percent provide full pay for a specified period followed by partial pay for the remaining leave time.

Waiting periods, ranging from one day to 10 days of absence before sick leave pay takes effect, are found in 30 percent of paid sick leave provisions. The most common period is one day, found in 41 percent of waiting period clauses, followed by two days stipulated in 28 percent.

Industry pattern: Paid sick leave provisions appear in more non-manufacturing agreements, 47 percent, than in manufacturing agreements, 23 percent. They are found in one-half or more of contracts in eight industries—utilities (80 percent), transportation (72 percent), communications (70 percent), services (63 percent), retail (59 percent), insurance and finance (57 percent), and chemicals and electrical machinery (each 50 percent). These provisions are absent from apparel, lumber, rubber, leather, maritime, and construction industry contracts.

Unpaid Sick Leave

Unpaid sick leave is provided in 53 percent of the contracts contained in the database. A length-of-service requirement is specified in 15 percent of these clauses. Of agreements containing length-of-service requirements, 23 percent specify one year, and 77 percent specify six months or less.

Duration of leave is discussed in 76 percent of unpaid sick leave clauses. Of these, 64 percent set a flat length of time ranging from one month to four years. One month, three months, six months, and one year are the most common periods of leave granted. Ten percent of provisions grant leave for the duration of an illness or until a doctor approves a return from leave. Length of leave is determined by an employee's length of service in 11 percent of clauses discussing duration.

Of unpaid sick leave provisions, 38 percent allow extension of the initial leave; 58 percent specify that a medical certification of illness or injury may be required.

Effect on seniority is discussed in 71 percent of unpaid sick leave provisions. Seniority accumulates for the full leave period under 60 percent of clauses mentioning the subject; seniority accumulates for a time and then is retained under 6 percent; seniority is retained for the entire period under 34 percent. Thirty-eight percent of seniority provisions place a limit on retention or accumulation.

Industry pattern: Unpaid sick leave provisions appear in 55 percent of manufacturing contracts and 49 percent of non-manufacturing agreements. Such leave is provided in all leather contracts and in two-thirds or more of sample contracts in rubber (83 percent), transportation (80 percent), transportation equipment (79 percent), services (78 percent), and textiles (70 percent). Unpaid sick leave is found in at least one-half of contracts in eight other industries.

Military Leave

Long-term military leave is mentioned in 66 percent of the sample. A bonus is paid upon entering military service in 9 percent of these clauses. Special provisions for returning disabled veterans are found in 14 percent of long-term military leave clauses; educational leave for veterans in 9 percent.

Short-term military leave for reserve training is mentioned in 38 percent of contracts analyzed. Pay while on short-term leave is discussed in 83 percent of these clauses. Of pay provisions, 91 percent guarantee the difference between regular pay and military pay. Length of leave is discussed in 81 percent of short-term leave provisions, with two weeks specified most frequently (70 percent).

Industry pattern: Military leave provisions appear in 81 percent of manufacturing agreements, 56 percent of non-manufacturing contracts, and in at least one-half of contracts in all industries except construction, apparel, maritime, and printing.

Leave of Absence Provisions

(Frequency Expressed as Percentage of Contracts in each Region*)

	Type of Leave								
	All Types	Person-al	Union	Family	Funeral	Civic	Paid Sick	Unpaid Sick	Mili-tary
All Regions	92	76	76	35	85	82	32	53	71
Middle Atlantic	92	78	76	37	89	83	43	50	76
Midwest	96	61	71	21	89	82	32	54	71
New England	89	81	73	42	89	77	46	54	73
North Central	96	83	85	38	93	91	19	60	75
Rocky Mountain	70	40	40	20	60	60	30	50	50
Southeast	96	72	85	32	83	87	26	43	79
Southwest	85	85	69	23	77	85	—	62	69
West Coast	80	73	49	29	71	62	47	42	38
Multiregion	94	79	89	42	83	81	37	60	83

* See p. xi for area designations.

11

Management and Union Rights

Management and union rights provisions are found in all the 400 sample contracts included in the Basic Patterns database.

Management rights generally are stated in a contract section labeled as such, while union rights usually are scattered throughout a contract according to subject matter.

Management rights statements are found in 79 percent of agreements analyzed. Of these, 77 percent reserve to the employer direction of the workforce, 74 percent management of the company business, 41 percent the right to frame company rules and 38 percent control of production methods.

Other designated prerogatives found in management clauses are: determining employees' duties, 27 percent; closing or relocating a plant, 16 percent; instituting technological changes, 13 percent.

Industry pattern: Management rights statements appear in 86 percent of manufacturing contracts and 69 percent of non-manufacturing agreements. They are found in all textiles, mining, insurance and finance, lumber, rubber, leather, and furniture contracts, and in at least 90 percent of chemicals, primary metals, fabricated metals, transportation equipment, and services agreements. In stone-clay-glass, services, electrical machinery, and machinery management rights are listed in from 85 percent to 89 percent of agreements studied. Further, management rights statements appear in 50 percent or more of contracts in the remaining industries with the exception of apparel, construction, and printing.

Management Rights Provisions

(Frequency Expressed as Percentage of Management Rights Statements)

	All Industries	Manufacturing	Non-manufacturing
Direct Work Force	77	77	77
Manage Business	74	76	69
Frame Company Rules	41	41	42
Control Production	38	48	17
Determine Employees' Duties	27	24	33
Close or Relocate Plant	16	17	12
Change Technology	13	16	8

Savings clauses appear in 44 percent of agreements, the same frequency as recorded in the 1989 study. They appear in 47 percent of manufacturing and 39 percent of non-manufacturing agreements. Of savings provisions, 60 percent state that management retains all rights not specifically modified or restricted by the contract; 62 percent state that management rights listed in the agreement are not necessarily all inclusive.

Restriction on Management Rights _____

Restrictions are placed on management in 88 percent of sample contracts—91 percent in manufacturing and 83 percent in non-manufacturing.
Fifty-five percent of agreements surveyed contain a general statement restricting management prerogatives. Of these, 97 percent prohibit management from taking actions in violation of the contract terms, and 16 percent
specify that management actions are subject to the grievance and/or arbitration procedure.

Industry pattern: Some restriction is placed on management rights in all
utilities, maritime, petroleum, rubber, apparel, mining, paper, and transportation equipment contracts. Such provisions are found in 90 percent or more
of communications, textiles, services, construction, stone-clay-glass, electrical machinery, and chemicals agreements. At least 80 percent of contracts in
all other industries except leather and printing (each 75 percent), transportation (68 percent), lumber (57 percent), and retail (56 percent) contain some
form of restriction on management rights.

Subcontracting is mentioned in 56 percent of the sample contracts—55
percent in manufacturing and 57 percent in non-manufacturing. In 48 percent of the subcontracting clauses, advance discussion with, or notification
to, the union is required; in 30 percent subcontracting is prohibited if layoffs
exist or would result from such action. Forty-one percent of these provisions
allow contracting out only if the necessary skills and equipment are not
available; 24 percent only if contractual standards are met. Under 17 percent
of subcontracting clauses, contracting out must be in accordance with past
practice.

Industry pattern: Limitations on contracting out are found in 100 percent
of apparel, 92 percent of mining, 90 percent of construction, 86 percent of
petroleum, 83 percent of rubber, 82 percent of transportation equipment, and
70 percent each of communications and utilities agreements. At least 50
percent of furniture, paper, primary metals, machinery, and services contracts contain subcontracting provisions.

Supervisory performance of bargaining unit work is limited in 58 percent of the sample contracts. Most of these clauses, however, provide that
work may be performed by supervisory employees on a limited basis under
one or more of the following conditions: for instruction purposes (75 percent), in case of emergency (71 percent), to conduct experiments (30 percent),
to develop new products (17 percent), and for demonstration purposes (15
percent). Twenty-three percent of the clauses limiting work by supervisors
allow them to work if a regular employee is not displaced, and 21 percent
specify for a limited time only. Work by non-union employees—for example,
management trainees—is permitted in 12 percent of contracts contained in
the sample database.

Industry pattern: Work by supervisors is limited in 74 percent of manufacturing agreements and 32 percent of non-manufacturing contracts. From 80 to 100 percent of furniture, mining, rubber, petroleum, machinery, paper, chemicals, primary metals, and transportation equipment agreements limit work by supervisors. Such limitations also are found in from 50 percent to 79 percent of lumber, apparel, communications, utilities, electrical machinery, fabricated metals, foods, textiles, leather, and stone-clay-glass contracts.

Restrictions on Management Rights

(Frequency Expressed as Percentage of Contracts)

	All Industries	Manufacturing	Non-manufacturing
General Statement	55	60	47
Subcontracting	56	55	57
Supervisory Performance of Work	58	74	32
Technological Changes	26	28	22
Plant Shutdown or Relocation	25	31	15

Technological changes are restricted in 26 percent of all contracts analyzed, and in 28 percent of manufacturing and 22 percent of non-manufacturing agreements. Of these provisions, 64 percent require advance discussion with, or notification to, the union and 18 percent (up from 12 percent in the 1989 study) state that the company will make an effort to retain displaced employees. In 27 percent of agreements limiting management's right to institute technological changes, retraining is required, and in 7 percent retraining is required only if an employee qualifies for the newly created job.

Industry pattern: Limitations on management's right to make technological changes are specified in 90 percent of communications, 89 percent of apparel, 88 percent of printing, 63 percent of maritime, 50 percent each of textiles and leather contracts, and in from 30 percent to 43 percent of rubber, petroleum, foods, retail, transportation equipment, and electrical machinery agreements.

Plant shutdown or relocation limitations are discussed in 25 percent of agreements analyzed. Advance notice to, or discussion with, the union is required under 72 percent of agreements dealing with the subject. In 42 percent of plant closure clauses, a displaced employee has transfer rights to a new location and in 24 percent the company is required to pay at least a portion of moving costs. Job placement and training programs are called for in 23 percent of shutdown provisions, while some other form of job security is found in 39 percent of the clauses.

Industry pattern: Shutdown and relocation provisions are found in 31 percent of manufacturing contracts and in 15 percent of non-manufacturing agreements. Such clauses appear in 89 percent of apparel, 67 percent of rubber, 60 percent of electrical machinery, 57 percent of petroleum, 50 percent of leather agreements, and in at least 40 percent of electrical machinery, and primary metals contracts. Further, these clauses appear in at least one-quarter of fabricated metals, foods, retail, mining, primary metals, and transportation equipment industry contracts.

Union Rights

Provisions stating union rights (use of bulletin boards, number of in-plant representatives, access to information, etc.) are found in 96 percent of contracts in the database—97 percent in manufacturing and 95 percent in non-manufacturing industry agreements.

Industry pattern: Union rights provisions appear in from 90 percent to 100 percent of all industry agreements except maritime (88 percent), lumber (86 percent), and utilities and transportation (each 80 percent).

In-plant union representatives are discussed in 54 percent of agreements studied—56 percent in manufacturing and 52 percent in non-manufacturing. Of these contracts, 24 percent specify how many stewards or committeemen are to represent a given number of employees in the bargaining unit, with varying limitations on the maximum number of representatives.

Access to plant by union representatives who are not company employees is permitted in 56 percent of agreements in the database—51 percent of manufacturing contracts and 63 percent of non-manufacturing agreements discuss the matter. A majority (87 percent) of access clauses either prohibit union representatives from interfering with production and/or require notification to management of their visit.

Union access to bulletin boards is specified in 70 percent of sample agreements—80 percent in manufacturing contracts and 52 percent in non-manufacturing contracts. In 66 percent of these provisions, the company furnishes the bulletin board, in 17 percent the union shares space with the company, in 7 percent the union furnishes its own, and in the remaining 10 percent it is unclear who furnishes the board.

Industry pattern: Bulletin board provisions are found in all rubber, textiles, and insurance and finance agreements, and in from 80 percent to 95 percent of mining, furniture, chemicals, petroleum, communications, utilities, lumber, electrical machinery, fabricated metals, machinery, paper, transportation equipment, and stone-clay-glass contracts. At least one-half of agreements in foods, leather, primary metals, retail, services, and transportation industries contain bulletin board clauses.

Restrictions on the use of bulletin boards are listed in 93 percent of agreements containing bulletin board provisions. The most common restrictions found in these clauses are use only for union business (83 percent), management approval of all postings (42 percent), and management approval of other than routine postings (16 percent). In from 8 percent to 14 percent of contracts restricting union use of bulletin boards, the union is prohibited from posting anything political, controversial, or derogatory to the company.

Union's right to information (other than data such as seniority lists) is stated in 61 percent of the sample—53 percent in manufacturing and 74 percent in non-manufacturing contracts. Of these provisions, 62 percent require that the union be notified of newly hired employees or of the need for additional employees, 23 percent specify that the union be given access to information on wages, and 15 percent permit union access to personnel data. Sixty-four percent of these clauses guarantee unions the right to various other information.

Union labels or store cards or decals are called for in 9 percent of the sample contracts. Such provisions are found in 89 percent of apparel contracts and in 44 percent of retail agreements.

Union Rights and Restrictions

(Frequency Expressed as Percentage of Contracts)

	All Industries	Manufacturing	Non-manufacturing
Access by Union Representatives	56	51	63
Bulletin Board Rights	70	80	52
Access to Information	61	53	74
Union Activity on Company Time			
No Union Activity	22	28	12
No Solicitation of Membership	16	22	7
No Dues Collection	8	11	3
No Distribution of Literature	7	8	5

Restricted Rights

Union activity on company time is specifically limited in 35 percent of agreements analyzed—44 percent in manufacturing and 21 percent in non-manufacturing. Of these agreements, 62 percent include a blanket prohibition of "union activity," 46 percent prohibit solicitation of union members, 24 percent prohibit dues collection, and 19 percent prohibit distribution of union literature on company time. Other forms of union activity are forbidden in 7 percent of agreements dealing with the subject.

Union business procedures are mentioned in 13 percent of contracts contained in the database, most notably in the construction industry (79 percent). Of these provisions, 64 percent include settlement procedures in instances of jurisdictional disputes and 52 percent ban strikes during jurisdictional disputes.

Management and Union Rights Provisions

(Frequency Expressed as Percentage of Contracts in Each Region*)

	Middle Atlantic	Midwest	New England	North Central	Rocky Mountain	Southeast	Southwest	West Coast	Multiregion
Management Rights	74	86	77	90	90	94	77	62	65
To Direct Working Force	50	71	58	72	90	79	62	44	46
To Manage Company Business	56	71	65	67	80	72	38	31	48
To Frame Company Rules	34	36	19	45	30	36	31	18	21
Restrictions on Management Rights	89	89	92	91	90	77	92	80	90
To Subcontract	59	39	50	54	60	55	69	51	69
To Close or Relocate Plant	21	14	31	29	20	9	15	13	54
To Implement New Technology	29	29	39	14	—	19	15	29	44
Union Rights	98	96	100	95	90	92	100	98	98
To Bulletin Boards	66	71	73	78	40	79	77	49	69
To Information	66	57	62	51	70	49	39	78	75
To Plant Entry By Union Officers	54	43	65	39	70	55	69	87	58
Restrictions on Union Rights (on company time)	37	36	23	41	10	55	39	11	33
Ban on Any Union Activity	26	21	4	30	10	36	15	7	13
Ban on Dues Collection	9	11	8	8	—	13	15	4	6
Ban on Solicitation of Membership	16	25	15	19	—	19	31	4	15

* See p. xi for area designations.

Union-Management Cooperation

Union-management cooperation pledges are found in 57 percent of contracts studied—up from 53 percent in the 1989 study, 45 percent in the 1986 study, 37 percent in the 1983 study, and 25 percent in the 1979 study. Of these provisions, 35 percent call for formation of joint committees to explore specific problems, such as absenteeism or productivity. Eighteen percent of the clauses stipulate establishment of joint committees to explore "mutual interests" (other than safety and health benefits), while 73 percent contain pledges of joint effort toward overall cooperation.

Some type of quality of worklife program is found in 28 of the 400 sample contracts, a steady climb from 25 recorded in the 1989 study, 17 recorded in the 1986 report, and nine recorded in the 1983 analysis.

Industry pattern: Provisions for union-management cooperation are found in 58 percent of manufacturing agreements and 56 percent of non-manufacturing contracts. From 64 percent to 100 percent of paper, apparel, stone-clay-glass, utilities, mining, primary metals, rubber, lumber, leather, furniture, maritime, transportation, and electrical machinery agreements contain cooperation clauses. Further, these provisions appear in at least one-half of communications, transportation equipment, foods, and services agreements.

12

Seniority

Seniority provisions, defined as employment service credit, are found in 90 percent of contracts in the Basic Patterns database—98 percent of manufacturing contracts and 77 percent of non-manucfaturing. Seniority is used most often to determine an employee's ranking for purposes of layoff (see Promotion and Transfer in this chapter).

Geographic analysis reveals that seniority is discussed in from 70 percent of contracts in the Rocky Mountain region to 98 percent of contracts in the Southeast region.

In 91 percent of contracts containing seniority provisions, seniority is based entirely on the length of an employee's continuous service. Three percent of these provisions define seniority as a combination of length of service and job qualifications, such as ability and fitness.

Probationary periods are required under 83 percent of sample contracts. Employees must complete these trial periods before they attain seniority rights. Of contracts requiring probationary periods, 77 percent state that the employer retains full authority to discipline or discharge employees during such time.

The most prevalent durations specified in probationary period provisions are 90 days (25 percent), 60 days (22 percent), 30 days (17 percent), 45 days (9 percent), 180 days (7 percent), and 120 days (5 percent). At the end of the trial period, an employee's seniority dates back to the date of hire.

Industry pattern: Probationary periods are contained in all contracts in chemicals, fabricated metals, furniture, lumber, machinery, petroleum, primary metals, rubber, stone-clay-glass, and textiles. In addition, such clauses appear in at least two-thirds of sample agreements in every industry except construction, maritime, and printing.

Probationary Periods

(Frequency Expressed as Percentage of Provisions)

	Number of Provisions	30 Days	45 Days	60 Days	90 Days	180 Days
All Industries	333	17	9	22	25	7
Manufacturing	227	15	11	23	26	5
Non-manufacturing	106	21	6	20	23	10

Loss of seniority is discussed in 80 percent of agreements studied—90 percent in manufacturing and 65 percent in non-manufacturing. Of these clauses, 92 percent state that seniority is lost after long-term layoff. Under contracts specifying loss of seniority after layoff, 54 percent specify that seniority is lost after a uniform length of time, and 46 percent key retention of seniority to an employee's length of service.

Reasons for loss of seniority other than lengthy layoff frequently are included in agreements. Under contracts dealing with seniority loss, 81 percent revoke seniority for failure to respond to recall; 51 percent for unauthorized absence; 45 percent for failure to report after leave of absence expiration; 29 percent after sickness or disability leave expires; and 16 percent for taking another job while on leave.

Seniority lists are required in 68 percent of contracts in the database—80 percent in manufacturing and 49 percent in non-manufacturing. Of these provisions, 47 percent require that lists be posted, and 76 percent require that the union be given copies. Management is committed to periodically revise the list under 81 percent of the clauses. Twenty-five percent of the provisions permit the union or the employee to protest lists, most often within 30 days.

Industry pattern: Seniority lists are mentioned in all contracts in furniture, petroleum, rubber, and textiles, and in at least two-thirds of the contracts in every industry except apparel, construction, insurance and finance, leather, maritime, printing, retail, services, stone-clay-glass, and utilities.

Seniority Provisions

(Frequency Expressed as Percentage of Contracts in Each Region*)

	Seniority Lists	Probationary Period	Loss of Seniority	Consideration of Seniority in Promotion	Consideration of Seniority in Transfer	Trial Period in New Job
All Regions	68	83	80	72	59	56
Middle Atlantic	60	79	77	73	52	54
Midwest	71	82	82	75	75	54
New England	65	81	69	58	58	58
North Central	80	91	89	78	72	68
Rocky Mountain	40	70	70	40	20	40
Southeast	83	94	85	89	62	66
Southwest	77	85	85	85	77	77
West Coast	40	73	71	56	36	36
Multiregion	71	79	79	65	54	42

* See p. xi for area designations.

Promotion

Seniority is assigned a role in determining promotions in 72 percent of the contracts studied—81 percent in manufacturing and 58 percent in non-manufacturing.

Seniority is the sole factor in promotions in 4 percent of sample contracts.

Seniority is the determining factor in promoting employees in 38 percent of the agreements. Under these, the most senior employees are promoted if they are qualified for the available job.

Seniority is a secondary factor to be considered only when other factors are equal in 27 percent of sample contracts.

Seniority is given equal consideration with other factors in determining promotions in only four contracts.

Industry pattern: Clauses specifying seniority as a factor in promotion appear in at least two-thirds of agreements in all industries except apparel, construction, maritime, printing, retail, and rubber.

Consideration of Seniority in Promotion

(Frequency Expressed as Percentage of Provisions)

	Number of Provisions	Sole Factor	Determining Factor	Secondary Factor	Equal With Other Factors
All Industries	288	6	52	38	1
Manufacturing	198	6	54	36	1
Non-manufacturing	90	4	48	42	2

Posting of Vacancies

Job vacancies must be posted, usually for a specified period of time, under 67 percent of contracts in the database. Posting provisions are found in 74 percent of manufacturing agreements and 56 percent of non-manufacturing contracts. Bidding procedures are included in 64 percent of sample agreements. A time limit within which bids must be submitted is specified in 67 percent of bidding clauses.

Trial periods on new jobs are called for in 56 percent of sample contracts.

Industry pattern: Provisions requiring that job vacancies be posted are found in at least one-half of the contracts in all industries except apparel, construction, maritime, printing, retail, and transportation equipment.

Transfer

Seniority is considered in granting employees' requests for transfers under 59 percent of the sample agreements—68 percent in manufacturing contracts and 43 percent in non-manufacturing.

Seniority is the sole factor in granting employees' requests for transfers in only 6 percent of contracts analyzed.

Seniority is the determining factor in transfers under 34 percent of the agreements. Under these provisions, senior employees are permitted to transfer if they can do the job.

Seniority is a secondary factor in granting requests for transfers in 16 percent of the sample. Such clauses consider seniority when other factors, such as qualifications, are equal.

Seniority is given equal consideration with other factors in authorizing transfers in only five contracts.

Industry pattern: Seniority is considered in granting requests for transfers in at least two-thirds of contracts in chemicals, communications, electrical machinery, fabricated metals, furniture, lumber, machinery, mining, paper, primary metals, rubber, textiles, transportation, transportation equipment, and utilities.

Consideration of Seniority in Transfer

(Frequency Expressed as Percentage of Provisions)

	Number of Provisions	Sole Factor	Determining Factor	Secondary Factor	Equal With Other Factors
All Industries	234	9	57	27	2
Manufacturing	167	8	59	26	2
Non-manufacturing	67	12	54	31	2

Temporary transfer provisions appear in 55 percent of sample contracts. These clauses are found in 68 percent of manufacturing agreements and 33 percent of those in non-manufacturing. In 67 percent of these provisions, temporary transfers are determined solely by management and in 66 percent a limit on duration is imposed.

Special transfer rights for disabled or aged employees, no longer able to perform their regular work, are called for in 34 percent of agreements—43 percent in manufacturing and 18 percent in non-manufacturing.

Effect of Transfers on Seniority Status

Seniority upon transfer from one department to another is considered in 26 percent of contracts in the database. Under 28 percent of these provisions, seniority is carried to the new department immediately, under 43 percent seniority is retained in the old department for a specified period, and under 29 percent of the clauses, seniority is carried to the new department after a time.

Seniority upon transfer from the bargaining unit—other than to supervisory positions—is dealt with in 45 percent of contracts studied. The subject is covered in 55 percent of manufacturing agreements and 30 percent of non-manufacturing. Of these clauses, 19 percent permit employees to retain their bargaining unit seniority indefinitely and 32 percent allow seniority to be retained for a while and then lost. Seniority may be accumulated indefinitely under 11 percent of the clauses; for a time and then retained under 13 percent; for a time and then lost under 12 percent.

Industry pattern: Provisions dealing with the effect on an employee's seniority upon transfer out of the bargaining unit to a non-supervisory position are included in at least one-half of the contracts in chemicals, electrical machinery, fabricated metals, furniture, leather, machinery, mining, paper, primary metals, rubber, textiles, transportation, and transportation equipment.

Seniority Provisions

(Frequency Expressed as Percentage of Industry Contracts)

	Proba-tionary Periods	Lists Re-quired	Vacan-cies Posted	Factor In:			Status Upon Transfer To:	
				Promo-tions	Layoffs	Trans-fers	Non-bargain-ing	Super-visory Job
ALL INDUSTRIES	83	68	67	72	88	59	45	28
MANUFACTUR-ING	93	80	74	81	96	68	55	37
Apparel	89	—	11	22	67	11	—	—
Chemicals	100	75	81	100	100	75	50	50
Electrical Machin-ery	75	70	75	75	100	75	70	30
Fabricated Metals	100	95	79	68	100	74	79	37
Foods	95	76	90	86	100	62	43	19
Furniture	100	100	83	83	100	83	50	50
Leather	75	25	50	75	100	25	75	50
Lumber	100	71	100	100	100	71	29	29
Machinery	100	96	100	85	100	85	77	31
Paper	93	71	71	100	93	93	50	50
Petroleum	100	100	71	100	100	43	—	43
Primary Metals	100	96	92	92	96	72	56	32
Printing	25	50	38	38	100	38	—	13
Rubber	100	100	83	50	83	83	67	50
Stone-Clay-Glass	100	62	85	92	100	54	46	46
Textiles	100	100	80	80	100	70	60	30
Transportation Equipment	91	88	35	79	91	68	68	56
NON-MANUFAC-TURING	68	49	56	58	74	43	30	13
Communications	70	70	80	70	100	80	30	30
Construction	3	—	—	—	3	—	—	—
Insurance & Fi-nance	71	57	86	71	71	29	43	—
Maritime	38	25	—	13	50	—	13	13
Mining	83	83	100	100	83	75	75	33
Retail	96	59	41	56	96	15	30	4
Services	89	44	78	78	93	63	26	—
Transportation	88	84	72	76	96	68	56	40
Utilities	80	40	100	100	90	100	20	10

Seniority and Supervisory Jobs _____

Seniority status of bargaining unit employees promoted to supervisory jobs is considered in 28 percent of agreements in the database—37 percent in manufacturing contracts and 13 percent in non-manufacturing.

Of these provisions, 17 percent allow indefinite accumulation of seniority while outside the unit, 13 percent specify that seniority is accumulated for a limited time and then lost, and 15 percent allow seniority to be accumulated for a time and then retained. Seniority is retained under 19 percent of the clauses, is retained for a limited time but then lost under 28 percent, and is lost immediately upon transfer to a supervisory job under 3 percent.

Industry pattern: The effect on an employee's seniority upon promotion to a supervisory position is not discussed in any apparel, construction, insurance and finance, or services contracts, but is discussed in at least one-half of those in chemicals, furniture, leather, paper, rubber, and transportation equipment.

13

Strikes and Lockouts

Strike and lockout provisions appear in 96 percent of the 400 sample agreements found in CBNC's Basic Patterns database and are somewhat more common in contracts in manufacturing industries (98 percent) than in non-manufacturing industries (94 percent). Geographic analysis shows that such clauses are contained in from 90 percent to 100 percent of contracts in areas designated in the database.

No-strike pledges

No-strike pledges are found in 95 percent of all agreements surveyed, falling into two general categories: 1) unconditional bans on interference with production during the life of the contract; and 2) conditional bans which permit strikes under certain circumstances. A no-strike ban most commonly is lifted after exhaustion of the grievance procedure, after an arbitration award has been violated, and/or over non-compliance with a contract provision.

Unconditional strike bans appear in 63 percent of sample agreements; conditional bans 31 percent.

No-Strike Pledges

(Frequency Expressed as Percentage of Contracts)

	All Industries	Manu-facturing	Non-manu-facturing
Unconditional Pledges	63	65	59
Conditional Pledges Waived After:			
Exhaustion of			
Grievance Procedure	10	11	8
Violation of Arbitration Award	11	11	12
Company Refusal to Arbitrate	5	4	5
Non-compliance With			
Portion of Contract	11	5	19
Reopener Impasse	1	2	1
Issues Outside			
Grievance Procedure	2	2	1
Other	9	9	8

Industry pattern: No-strike pledges are found in 97 percent of manufacturing contracts and in 92 percent of non-manufacturing agreements. All contracts in 14 industries include a no-strike pledge—textiles, petroleum, apparel, lumber, furniture, paper, leather, rubber, electrical machinery, maritime, foods, stone-clay-glass, construction, and utilities. Three-quarters or more of contracts in every other industry have such a provision.

Unconditional pledges are found in one-half or more of the contracts in 21 industries, appearing in more than three-quarters of agreements in paper and leather (each 100 percent); utilities (90 percent); maritime (88 percent); lumber and insurance and finance (each 86 percent); stone-clay-glass (85 percent); furniture and mining (each 83 percent); machinery and retail (each 81 percent); and primary metals (80 percent).

Conditional no-strike pledges appear with the same frequency—31 percent—in non-manufacturing agreements and in manufacturing agreements. These clauses appear in one-half or more of contracts in apparel (89 percent),construction (86 percent), petroleum (71 percent), textiles (60 percent), and electrical machinery (50 percent). No-strike bans may be lifted for the following reasons:

Exhaustion of grievance procedure: Thirty-one percent of conditional bans are lifted for this reason. The waiver is found in 13 of the 26 industries researched, and mainly in transportation, electrical machinery, transportation equipment, and construction.

Violation of arbitration award: No-strike bans lifted for this reason are found in 36 percent of sample contracts with conditional bans. This waiver appears most often in apparel, electrical machinery, construction, foods, services, and transportation.

Company refusal to arbitrate dispute: Fourteen percent of the contracts with conditional bans allow strikes in this situation. Eleven of the 26 industries studied have at least one contract with such a provision, but no industry has a concentration.

Non-compliance with portion of agreement: Thirty-four percent of conditional bans are lifted for this reason. Eleven industries have at least one contract with such a clause, but the provision is concentrated in agreements in only two industries—apparel (78 percent) and construction (69 percent).

Deadlocked contract reopener: Strikes are permitted in this circumstance in only 4 percent of contracts with conditional no-strike pledges, occurring most frequently in the textiles (20 percent) and petroleum (14 percent) industries.

Issues outside grievance procedure: Only 5 percent of conditional bans are waived for this reason.

Strike and Lockout Provisions

(Frequency Expressed as Percentage of Contracts in Each Region*)

	Middle Atlantic	Midwest	New England	North Central	Rocky Mountain	Southeast	Southwest	West Coast	Multiregion
Provisions	96	93	96	97	100	98	100	98	90
No Strike Pledge	95	93	96	96	100	94	100	98	90
Unconditional	67	57	65	70	60	68	46	62	46
Conditional	28	36	31	24	40	26	54	33	44
No Lockout Pledge	92	93	85	90	100	92	92	89	89
Unconditional	73	71	73	72	90	75	62	62	58
Conditional	21	21	12	17	10	13	31	24	31
Union Strike Liability	37	50	54	45	20	70	39	16	39
Definition of Authorized Strike	9	14	12	10	—	11	—	2	15
Penalties for Strikers	34	50	42	50	10	70	46	31	44
Other Employees Access to Plant During Strike	2	4	4	1	10	9	15	4	2
Non-Striking Employees May Observe Picket Line	20	25	27	18	60	13	31	60	17
Struck Work Provisions	6	4	—	8	—	4	—	16	8

* See p. xi for area designations.

No-Lockout Pledges

No-lockout pledges appear in 90 percent of contracts in the database. These provisions usually contain language similar, if not identical, to that found in no-strike pledges. Unconditional pledges appear in 70 percent of the sample; conditional pledges in 20 percent.

Industry pattern: No-lockout pledges appear in 93 percent of manufacturing agreements and in 86 percent of non-manufacturing contracts. All textiles, apparel, lumber, furniture, maritime, petroleum, electrical machinery, leather, stone-clay-glass, utilities, and rubber agreements contain no-lockout pledges. In addition, they appear in at least 83 percent of all contracts in every other industry, with the exception of communications (70 percent) and transportation (64 percent).

No-Lockout Pledges
(Frequency Expressed as Percentage of Contracts)

	All Industries	Manu-facturing	Non-manu-facturing
Unconditional Pledges	70	71	68
Conditional Pledges Waived After:			
Exhaustion of			
Grievance Procedure	8	9	7
Violation of Arbitration Award	7	7	6
Union Refusal to Arbitrate	3	2	3
Non-compliance With			
Portion of Contract	3	2	5
Reopener Impasse	1	1	—
Other	5	5	5

Unconditional bans appear in all contracts in rubber, leather, and maritime. Such provisions are found in one-half or more of agreements in every other industry except construction, transportation, and communications.

Conditional no-lockout pledges, appearing in 22 percent of manufacturing contracts and 17 percent of non-manufacturing contracts, may be waived for reasons similar to those that permit waiver of no-strike pledges, including the following:

Exhaustion of grievance procedure: This is the reason for waiver of the no-lockout pledge in 41 percent of contracts with such a provision. It is found in at least one contract in 11 of the 26 industries and occurs with greatest frequency in transportation equipment (29 percent), electrical machinery (20 percent), construction (17 percent), and transportation (16 percent) contracts.

Violation of arbitration award: Thirty-four percent of conditional bans may be waived for this reason. This waiver most often appears in agreements in apparel (33 percent) and foods (24 percent).

Union refusal to arbitrate dispute: Lockouts are allowed in this circumstance under 14 percent of contracts with conditional pledges. No single industry has a significant number of agreements with such a clause.

Non-compliance with portion of agreement: No-lockout bans are lifted for this reason in 15 percent of contracts with conditional pledges. Such provisions are not concentrated in any one industry.

Waivers for various other reasons appear in 24 percent of contracts with conditional no-lockout pledges.

Limitations on Union Liability

Provisions limiting a union's liability for violation of a no-strike pledge appear in 42 percent of agreements studied. Some form of positive action usually is required of the union to avoid liability. Of contracts with liability clauses, 83 percent require that the union attempt to get the employees to return to work and 30 percent specify that the union must publicly disavow the strike. Twenty-five percent of the provisions deny release of union liability if the work stoppage was initiated or encouraged by any union officer. Various other requirements of the union are found in 21 percent of these clauses. Further, many contracts specify more than one requirement of the union.

Some agreements approach the question of liability by specifying conditions under which a strike is authorized. Such statements appear in 10 percent of the sample and are more commonly found in manufacturing (12 percent) than in non-manufacturing (6 percent) agreements. Of these, 50 percent indicate who may or may not authorize a strike and 74 percent require approval from the international union.

The local union is exempt from responsibility for unauthorized strikes in 68 percent of liability clauses; the international union is exempt in 28 percent.

Union Avoidance of Strike Liability
(Frequency Expressed as Percentage of Contracts)

	All Industries	Manu-facturing	Non-manu-facturing
Liability Limited	42	50	30
Requirements Placed on Union:			
Strike Not Initiated by Officers	11	12	9
Must Order Work Resumed	35	41	26
Must Disavow Strike	13	14	10
Other	9	8	11

Industry pattern: Provisions limiting union liability are more common in manufacturing (50 percent) than in non-manufacturing (30 percent) agreements. Such clauses appear in all textiles and rubber agreements and in one-half or more of those in apparel, furniture, fabricated metals, leather, stone-clay-glass, paper, insurance and finance, utilities, mining, and chemicals.

Penalties for Strikers

Discipline or discharge of employees participating in illegal strikes is permitted in 45 percent of agreements in the sample database. Of these, 42 percent provide for appeal from the penalty imposed, although 56 percent of agreements permitting appeal limit it to the question of participation in the strike.

Industry pattern: Provisions allowing penalties for illegal strikes are far more common in manufacturing (55 percent) than in non-manufacturing (28 percent) contracts. All furniture and textiles agreements contain such a provision. One-half or more of the contracts in 11 other industries—rubber (83 percent), transportation equipment (74 percent), apparel (67 percent), maritime (63 percent), paper (57 percent), primary metals (56 percent), electrical machinery (55 percent), and machinery, mining, utilities, and leather (each 50 percent)—have such clauses.

Appeals are permitted in 46 percent of manufacturing agreements containing penalty provisions and in 32 percent of non-manufacturing contracts with such clauses. These provisions are most common in contracts in furniture (83 percent) and textiles (80 percent), and are found in one-fourth or more of the agreements in electrical machinery, transportation equipment, leather, stone-clay-glass, and primary metals.

Picket Lines and Struck Work

Twenty-five percent of contracts studied state that employees may observe picket lines in certain situations. As a general rule, picket lines must be primary and legal to be considered within the purview of such provisions. Of agreements with such clauses, 11 percent allow observance of a picket line only at the employees' own plant; 75 percent allow observance at any plant; and 14 percent allow observance if certain other conditions are met, such as approval of the strike by the local central labor body. Three contracts permit observance only if the line is manned by the employees' own union.

Provisions allowing observance of picket lines are far more common in non-manufacturing (43 percent) than in manufacturing (13 percent) contracts. Picket line clauses are found in 70 percent of contracts in retail, 78 percent in apparel, 63 percent in maritime, 60 percent in communications, 62 percent in construction, and 52 percent in services.

Struck-work clauses appear in 7 percent of the sample, and in 7 percent each in manufacturing and non-manufacturing agreements. Of the 27 contracts containing struck-work provisions, 16 allow employees to refuse to handle only goods struck by their own union, while 11 permit employees to refuse to handle any struck goods. Employer pledges not to accept struck goods are found in only eight of the sample contracts.

Access to the plant during a strike by non-striking employees is guaranteed in 4 percent of agreements included in the database. Such guarantees most often apply to maintenance and security personnel.

Union Security

Union security provisions, including check-off and hiring arrangements, are found in all but one of the agreements contained in the Basic Patterns database. Geographic analysis shows that such clauses are contained in from 98 to 100 percent of contracts in regions designated in the database.

Eighty-three percent of the contracts analyzed provide for one or more of the principal forms of union security—union shop, modified union shop, maintenance-of-membership, and agency shop. Check-off provisions appear in 96 percent of the sample; hiring provisions in 22 percent.

Union shop is by far the most prevalent form of security. Provided in 62 percent of the sample, union shop clauses require that all employees in the bargaining unit become members and maintain membership as a condition of employment.

Industry pattern: At least three-fourths of contracts in apparel, construction, furniture, printing, retail, and rubber contain union shop provisions. Such provisions are absent in petroleum agreements analyzed and appear in less than 50 percent of those in primary metals (48 percent), lumber (43 percent), utilities (40 percent), communications and textiles (each 30 percent), and mining (17 percent).

Modified union shop provisions are found in 13 percent of sample agreements. Of the various forms of modification, the most common requires union membership of all employees except those who were not members on or before the contract's effective date or another specified date. In a few agreements, groups such as temporary workers and religious objectors are excused from the membership requirement.

Industry pattern: Modified union shop provisions are found in 32 percent of primary metals agreements, 25 percent each of electrical machinery and mining, 24 percent of foods, 23 percent of machinery, and 20 percent of utilities. This type of provision does not appear in any apparel, furniture, leather, lumber, petroleum, printing, rubber, or textiles industries agreements studied.

Agency shop, which requires payment of service fees—usually equal in amount to union dues—by employees who choose not to join the union, is found in 11 percent of contracts analyzed. In 4 percent of the sample, agency shop exists as the sole form of union security. The remaining 7 percent of agency shop provisions are found in contracts covering multistate operations—almost three-fourths (74 percent) appear in combination with union shop and the other more than one-fourth (26 percent) with modified union shop. In such instances, agency shop is applicable, to the extent that it is lawful, in states that prohibit compulsory union membership.

Industry pattern: Agency shop provisions (as the sole form of union security) appear in 40 percent of communications, 17 percent of furniture, 13 percent of maritime, 12 percent of transportation contracts, and in 10 percent of utilities agreements in the database.

Union Security Provisions

(Frequency Expressed as Percentage of Contracts)

	Union Shop	Modi-fied Union Shop	Agency Shop Only	Main-tenance of Member-ship	Hiring	Check-off
ALL INDUSTRIES	62	13	4	3	22	96
MANUFACTURING	61	14	2	3	10	98
Apparel	89	—	—	—	33	100
Chemicals	56	13	—	13	6	100
Electrical Machinery	70	25	—	—	5	100
Fabricated Metals	53	16	5	11	5	95
Foods	62	24	—	5	24	100
Furniture	83	—	17	—	—	100
Leather	50	—	—	—	25	100
Lumber	43	—	—	—	—	100
Machinery	65	23	8	—	—	100
Paper	57	14	—	7	—	100
Petroleum	—	—	—	14	14	100
Primary Metals	48	32	—	—	—	100
Printing	88	—	—	—	75	75
Rubber	83	—	—	—	—	100
Stone, Clay, & Glass	69	15	—	—	8	100
Textiles	30	—	—	10	—	90
Transportation Equipment	71	3	3	—	12	100
NON-MANUFACTURING	65	11	7	3	42	92
Communications	30	10	40	—	10	100
Construction	83	10	—	—	90	76
Insurance & Finance	57	14	—	14	—	100
Maritime	50	13	13	13	100	63
Mining	17	25	—	—	—	100
Retail	89	7	—	—	41	96
Services	70	7	7	7	56	96
Transportation	64	8	12	—	8	100
Utilities	40	20	10	10	20	100

Maintenance-of-membership provisions, requiring present union members to so remain but imposing no obligation on non-members, appear in only 3 percent of sample agreements.

Industry pattern: Maintenance-of-membership provisions are found in 14 percent each of petroleum and insurance and finance contracts, 13 percent each of chemicals and maritime agreements, and in at least 10 percent of fabricated metals, textiles, and utilities agreements.

Right-to-work laws, prohibiting compulsory union membership (in effect in 21 states), influence union security provisions in 26 percent of contracts in the database. Fifteen percent of contracts analyzed cover bargaining units located wholly in right-to-work states; the other 11 percent cover multistate units, some of which are located in right-to-work states. Further, 5 percent of the contracts surveyed either call for a first union security provision or a stronger provision than that already appearing in the contract should right-to-work or other limiting laws be repealed.

Because of the legal restrictions in many states, a geographic analysis reveals wide variations in the frequency of union shop provisions. Inclusion of these clauses ranges from 15 percent in the Southeast and Southwest regions to 84 percent on the West Coast. Check-off provisions, on the other hand, are prevalent in all regions and range from 91 percent of West Coast contracts to 100 percent of Rocky Mountain agreements.

Union Security Provisions

(Frequency Expressed as Percentage of Contracts in Each Region*)

	Union Shop	Modified Union Shop	Agency Shop Only	Maintenance of Member-ship	Hiring	Check-off
All Regions	62	13	4	3	22	96
Middle Atlantic	71	18	1	4	21	98
Midwest	61	7	4	4	18	93
New England	65	19	4	–	27	92
North Central	69	18	7	2	10	99
Rocky Mountain	80	–	–	–	30	100
Southeast	15	2	–	9	13	96
Southwest	15	8	–	–	23	92
West Coast	84	9	4	2	60	91
Multiregion	67	12	8	4	21	96

* See p. xi for area designations.

Hiring Arrangements

Hiring provisions are found in 22 percent of contracts in the database—10 percent in manufacturing and 42 percent in non-manufacturing.

Industry pattern: Hiring provisions are found in all maritime agreements analyzed, and in 90 percent of construction, 75 percent of printing, 56 percent of services, 41 percent of retail, and in at least 25 percent of apparel and leather agreements.

Hiring-preference provisions, requiring that preference in employment be given to workers in the area and/or to those with experience in the industry, are found in 39 percent of contracts with hiring provisions, or in 9 percent of the entire sample.

Industry pattern: Provisions for preference in hiring are most common in construction (55 percent) and maritime and printing (each 25 percent) contracts. Such clauses also appear in at least 10 percent of apparel, communications, utilities, services, and foods industry agreements.

Hiring procedures, referring to a union role in furnishing candidates for employment, are found in 21 percent of the database—9 percent in manufacturing and 41 percent in non-manufacturing. Of these provisions, 94 percent call for union operation of a hiring hall; the remainder call for a joint labor-management operation. In many cases, however, the employer may seek job applicants from other sources either simultaneously or after the union has been given the first opportunity to supply candidates.

Industry pattern: Hiring hall provisions are found in 90 percent of construction, 88 percent of maritime, 75 percent of printing, 56 percent of services, 41 percent of retail, and 33 percent of apparel agreements.

Check-off

Provisions for check-off are contained in 96 percent of contracts studied—98 percent of manufacturing and 92 percent of non-manufacturing agreements.

Industry pattern: Check-off provisions appear in all contracts in the apparel, chemicals, communications, electrical machinery, foods, furniture, insurance and finance, leather, lumber, machinery, mining, paper, petroleum, primary metals, rubber, stone-clay-glass, transportation, transportation equipment, and utilities industries. Further, these provisions are found in at least 63 percent of contracts in all other industries analyzed.

Items to be deducted are specified in all contracts containing check-off provisions. Of these agreements, only two do not mention union dues as an item to be deducted; 79 percent mention initiation fees; 28 percent mention assessments; 20 percent mention political action contributions; and 17 percent mention other fees such as reinstatement and/or agency fees. A contract may provide for only one type of deduction or may permit a combination of the specified deductions.

Amounts to be deducted are referred to in 11 percent of contracts containing check-off provisions. Of these, more than three-fourths (81 percent) specify a fixed amount of dues to be deducted, and the other 20 percent place limitations on deductions.

Revocation of check-off authorization is mentioned in 47 percent of sample agreements providing for check-off. Of these, 82 percent hold authorizations to be irrevocable for the term of the contract or one year, whichever is shorter, and 14 percent allow employees to revoke at any time or upon short notice.

Automatic renewal of check-off authorization takes place if an employee fails to cancel under 76 percent of irrevocable check-off provisions. In 93 percent of these cases, the renewed authorization continues to be irrevocable for specified periods, and in the remaining 7 percent it continues on a revoca ble basis. Authorizations revocable from the outset remain in effect until cancelled; therefore renewal problems do not arise.

Escape periods, during which resignation from check-off and/or union membership is permitted, are specified in 32 percent of sample agreements—40 percent in manufacturing and 20 percent in non-manufacturing. These provisions are found in 83 percent of rubber contracts, and in at least 50 percent of chemicals, insurance and finance, paper, textiles, and transportation equipment agreements.

Frequency of Check-off Provisions

(Frequency Expressed as Number of Contracts)

	All Industries	Manu- facturing	Non-manu- facturing
Provision for Authorized Check-off	384	241	143
Type of Authorization:			
Revocable at Will	26	10	16
Irrevocable for Contract Term or One Year	149	114	35
Automatic Renewal*			
Becomes Revocable	8	6	2
Continues Irrevocable	105	87	18
Deductions in Addition to Dues			
Assessments	108	61	47
Initiation Fees	305	203	102
Political Action Contributions	77	45	32

*After "escape" period.

15

Vacations

Vacation provisions are found in 91 percent of all 400 contracts in CBNC's Basic Patterns database, and in 98 percent of all agreements outside the construction industry. Geographical analysis shows that such provisions are contained in from 70 percent to 98 percent of contracts in areas designated in the database.

Vacation provisions are absent in all but one construction agreement and in only seven contracts in all other industries—three in maritime, two in apparel, and one each in transportation and transportation equipment.

Amount of Vacation

The latest survey reveals little change since the 1989 study in the percentage of sample contracts providing one, two, three, or four weeks of vacation. One-week vacations are less frequent than two-, three-, and four-week vacations because a number of contracts provide minimum vacations of two weeks or longer.

Five-week vacations appear in a majority of sample contracts, having risen in frequency from only 2 percent in the 1966 study to 62 percent in this year's survey. Six-week vacations have climbed steadily, increasing from 5 percent in the 1971 study to 22 percent in this year's analysis.

Trend in Amount of Vacation Per Year

(Frequency Expressed as Percentage of Contracts)

	1966	1971	1975	1979	1983	1986	1989	1992
Three weeks	84	86	85	86	87	89	89	88
Four weeks	50	73	76	79	83	84	85	86
Five weeks	2	22	42	53	58	62	61	62
Six weeks	—	5	10	16	20	22	21	22

Industry pattern: Vacations of up to six weeks are more prevalent in manufacturing than non-manufacturing principally because of the absence of vacation provisions in all but one construction contract. Vacations of more than six weeks, however, are slightly more prevalent in non-manufacturing. Four weeks is the maximum amount of vacation in apparel contracts.

Five weeks vacation is provided in all contracts in communications, paper, petroleum, rubber, and utilities and appears in at least two-thirds of contracts in eight other industries: chemicals, electrical machinery, foods, furniture, machinery, primary metals, retail, and transportation. Chemicals, maritime, paper, petroleum, rubber, transportation, and utilities are the only industries in which at least one-half of contracts grant six-week vacations.

Annual vacations of more than six weeks appear in only 12 contracts—five in transportation, three in paper, two in foods, and one each in communications and utilities.

Amount of Vacation

(Frequency Expressed as Percentage of Industry Contracts; Excludes Vacations Not Based on Length of Service)

	Percent of contracts providing vacations totaling:						
	1 week	2 weeks	3 weeks	4 weeks	5 weeks	6 weeks	more than 6 weeks
ALL INDUSTRIES	73	88	88	86	62	22	3
MANUFACTURING	79	96	96	94	66	23	2
Apparel	22	44	44	56	—	—	—
Chemicals	81	100	100	100	94	56	—
Electrical Machinery	80	95	100	100	90	15	—
Fabricated Metals	95	100	100	100	63	11	—
Foods	90	100	100	100	86	38	10
Furniture	100	100	100	100	67	—	—
Leather	100	100	100	100	25	25	—
Lumber	100	100	100	86	43	14	—
Machinery	88	96	100	100	73	8	—
Paper	100	100	100	100	100	100	21
Petroleum	14	100	100	100	100	100	—
Primary Metals	84	96	96	92	72	4	—
Printing	63	88	88	100	13	—	—
Rubber	33	100	100	100	100	100	—
Stone, Clay & Glass	92	100	100	85	54	8	—
Textiles	90	100	100	90	50	—	—
Transportation Equipment	65	94	91	88	41	6	—
NON-MANUFACTURING	64	76	75	72	54	21	5
Communications	90	90	100	100	100	10	10
Construction	—	—	—	—	—	—	—
Insurance & Finance	86	100	100	100	57	29	—
Maritime	50	50	50	38	38	50	—
Mining	58	92	83	75	58	—	—
Retail	93	100	100	96	74	11	—
Services	67	93	93	85	26	—	—
Transportation	84	96	92	92	92	64	20
Utilities	90	100	100	100	100	60	10

Amount of Vacation

(Frequency Expressed as Percentage of Contracts in Each Region*; Excludes Vacations Not Based on Length of Service)

	Percent of contracts providing vacations totaling:						
	1 week	2 weeks	3 weeks	4 weeks	5 weeks	6 weeks	more than 6 weeks
ALL REGIONS	73	88	88	86	62	22	3
Middle Atlantic	73	90	88	84	61	16	1
Midwest	79	86	89	93	54	18	4
New England	85	85	85	81	73	19	4
North Central	81	93	94	93	72	26	2
Rocky Mountain	40	70	70	70	50	20	—
Southeast	81	96	96	89	60	26	2
Southwest	54	85	77	77	54	23	—
West Coast	60	78	78	71	36	18	—
Multiregion	65	83	85	87	69	31	12

* See p. xi for area designations.

Vacation Based on Length of Service _____

Vacation entitlement is keyed to length of service under 89 percent of sample contracts in the database. The remaining 2 percent of contracts mentioning vacation either grant a standard amount of vacation to all employees regardless of service or spell out the amount of vacation pay but not the amount of vacation.

The median service requirement for specified amounts of vacation in the current survey is one year for one week, two years for two weeks, eight years for three weeks, 15 years for four weeks, 20.5 years for five weeks, and 28 years for six weeks.

One-week vacations are called for in 73 percent of the total sample. Twenty-eight percent of these provisions grant a vacation to employees with less than one year of service, while 72 percent require one full year of service. A week after less than one year is more common in non-manufacturing (35 percent) than in manufacturing (25 percent). Half or more of the contracts in communications, insurance and finance, maritime, printing, and utilities provide a week of vacation after less than one year of service.

Two-week vacations appear in 88 percent of contracts analyzed. Of these provisions, 7 percent require less than one year of service; 27 percent require one year. A majority of contracts in communications, insurance and finance, petroleum, printing, rubber, and utilities grant two weeks after a year or less of service.

Two years of service is the requirement for two-week vacations in 28 percent of two-week provisions. At least one-half of contracts in foods, leather, and retail specify two years of service.

Three years of service is the requirement in another 28 percent of two-week provisions, appearing in at least one-half the agreements in fabricated metals, furniture, mining, paper, and primary metals.

Four or five years of service are required in 10 percent of two-week provisions and are found more often in manufacturing (14 percent) than non-manufacturing (1 percent) agreements. A five-year requirement is found most frequently in the textiles industry.

Three-week vacations appear in 88 percent of the agreements. Seven percent of these provisions require less than five years of service; 26 percent require five years. All contracts in petroleum and more than one-half of those in chemicals, rubber, and transportation require five years of service.

Six to nine years is the most common requirement, appearing in 35 percent of contracts providing three weeks of vacation. At least 50 percent of all agreements in communications, paper, electrical machinery, and utilities require six to nine years for three weeks of vacation.

Ten years is the service requirement under 27 percent of three-week provisions and is found in at least one-half of fabricated metals, furniture, leather, and primary metals agreements.

Six percent of three-week provisions require 11 or more years of service.

Four-week vacations are provided under 86 percent of the database sample contracts, with service requirements ranging from one to 25 years. A requirement of less than 10 years appears in 7 percent of the provisions; a requirement of 10 years appears in 12 percent. All contracts in petroleum and printing and at least 50 percent of agreements in chemicals and transportation provide four weeks after 10 or fewer years. Fifteen percent of four-week provisions require 11 to 14 years of service.

A 15-year service requirement appears in 30 percent of contracts providing four-week vacations, including all rubber agreements and at least one-half of those in communications, insurance and finance, and utilities. A requirement of 16 to 19 years is found in 14 percent of these clauses and appears most frequently in mining and primary metals agreements.

Twenty years is the requirement in 19 percent of the four-week provisions, and 25 years is the requirement in 3 percent.

Five-week vacations appear in 62 percent of the contracts surveyed, and service requirements range from eight to 32 years. Five weeks are granted after less than 20 years in 16 percent of the provisions, while 20 years is the requirement in 34 percent. All petroleum agreements, and at least 50 percent of chemicals, paper, and rubber contracts, require 20 years for five weeks. Twenty-one to 24 years of service is required under 9 percent of five-week provisions.

Twenty-five years is the requirement under 37 percent of provisions granting five weeks of vacation. A 25-year service requirement is found in at least one-half of communications, furniture, insurance and finance, and primary metals agreements. Thirty years of service is required under 4 percent of five-week provisions.

Six-week vacations are provided in 22 percent of sample contracts. Of these provisions, 39 percent call for 30 years of service, 30 percent require 25 years, and the remainder require from eight to 35 years. All paper, petroleum, and rubber contracts provide six weeks of vacation. At least one-half of chemicals, maritime, transportation, and utilities contracts grant six-week vacations. Thirty years is the most common service requirement in chemicals, petroleum, and utilities; 25 years is the most common in foods and paper.

Vacation Service Requirements

(Frequency Expressed as Percentage of Contracts Granting Specified Amounts of Vacation*)

Service requirement	Amount of Vacation					
	1 week	2 weeks	3 weeks	4 weeks	5 weeks	6 weeks
Less than 1 year	28	7	1	—	—	—
1 year	72	27	2	1	—	—
2 years	—	29	2	—	—	—
3-4 years	—	30	2	1	—	—
5 years	—	7	26	3	—	—
6-9 years	—	—	35	3	—	1
10 years	—	—	27	12	1	—
11-14 years	—	—	2	15	2	3
15 years	—	—	4	30	5	2
16-19 years	—	—	—	14	9	—
20 years	—	—	—	19	34	5
21-24 years	—	—	—	—	9	6
25 years	—	—	—	3	37	30
26-29 years	—	—	—	—	—	11
30 years	—	—	—	—	4	39
31-34 years	—	—	—	—	—	—
35 years	—	—	—	—	—	2

* Because of rounding sums may not total 100.

Two-Tier Vacation Benefits

Twenty-four of the sample contracts in the 1992 survey provide reduced vacation benefits for new hires, up from 16 contracts analyzed in 1989 and four analyzed in 1986.

Under these provisions, new employees never gain eligibility for the maximum amount granted to senior workers, or are subjected to protracted length of service requirements to achieve maximum vacation benefits.

Eighteen manufacturing agreements and six non-manufacturing agreements have two-tier vacation provisions.

Partial and Interim Benefits

In addition to vacations in weekly periods, partial vacations for employees who do not qualify for a first full vacation are called for in 20 percent of the sample. Further, interim benefits for those between weeks of qualification are provided by 27 percent of the contracts. Interim benefits often consist of additional individual days of vacation or a higher rate of vacation pay.

Partial vacations are found in 22 percent of manufacturing agreements and 15 percent of non-manufacturing contracts. Interim benefits appear in 32 percent of manufacturing and 19 percent of non-manufacturing agreements. At least 50 percent of agreements in electrical machinery, furniture, insurance and finance, stone-clay-glass, transportation equipment, and utilities provide interim benefits.

Extended Vacations

Extended vacations appear in seven of the 400 sample contracts, up from six in 1989, but down from 10 in 1986 and 17 in 1983. The low number is largely due to elimination of extended vacation provisions in contracts negotiated by the United Steelworkers. Three provisions in the 1992 survey are in fabricated metals, and one each in chemicals, communications, textiles, and utilities.

The interval between extended vacations is four years in one plan and five years in the other six. The amount of vacation ranges from one week to 13 weeks.

Vacation Pay

Eighty-seven percent of database sample contracts state the basis on which vacation pay is to be computed. Fifty-three percent of these provide pay at base or straight time rates; 32 percent compute pay on an employee's average earnings, usually over the previous year; 8 percent compute pay on rates or averages, whichever is greater; and 7 percent compute pay on base rates or average earnings, depending on classification.

Inclusion of shift differentials in the computation of vacation pay is expressly called for under 24 percent of vacation pay provisions, while inclusion of overtime earnings is specified by 5 percent. In addition, many agreements basing vacation pay on average earnings state that vacation pay is a percentage of "all earnings."

Vacation bonus provisions appear in 7 percent of the sample. Some call for a flat vacation bonus, while others provide a specified amount for each week of vacation taken.

Industry pattern: Vacation pay is computed on the basis of straight-time rates in 76 percent of non-manufacturing agreements, compared with 42 percent of manufacturing contracts. All other methods of computing vacation pay, inclusion of shift differentials, and vacation bonuses are found more often in manufacturing than in non-manufacturing agreements.

Vacation Pay

(Frequency Expressed as Percentage of Vacation Pay Provisions)

	Based on Straight Time Rate	Based on Average Earnings	Either, Depending on Classification	Whichever is greater
All Industries	53	32	7	8
Manufacturing	42	38	8	12
Non-manufacturing	76	19	5	—

Vacation pay is computed on regular rates in two-thirds or more of agreements in chemicals, communications, printing, services, transportation, and utilities. It is based on average earnings in more than two-thirds of contracts in primary metals and rubber. Vacation bonuses appear most frequently in electrical machinery, fabricated metals, machinery, primary metals, and transportation equipment.

Work Requirements

To ensure that vacations are granted principally to employees who work a substantial portion of the year, many contracts condition vacation entitlement on a requirement that employees work a minimum time or percentage of available hours during the year. Fifty-five percent of all sample contracts contain a work requirement provision. These requirements are stated as a minimum number or amount of hours, days, weeks, months, or pay.

Less than one-half of a year is required in 16 percent of these provisions, one-half to three-quarters of a year is required in 55 percent, and more than three-quarters of a year is required in 30 percent. Of these requirements, 65 percent call for proration of vacation or vacation pay if the minimum work requirement is not met.

Industry pattern: Work requirements appear in 64 percent of manufacturing contracts and 41 percent of non-manufacturing agreements. Requirements usually are higher in non-manufacturing contracts, with 97 percent requiring one-half year or more, compared to 80 percent in manufacturing agreements.

More than two-thirds of contracts in fabricated metals, foods, furniture, leather, lumber, machinery, mining, primary metals, retail, stone-clay-glass, and transportation contain work requirements.

Among industries in which a majority of contracts contain such provisions, requirements are strictest in foods, mining, petroleum, retail, and transportation and are less strict in electrical machinery, machinery, and stone-clay-glass.

No reduction in full vacation entitlement is imposed for time lost for a variety of reasons under 55 percent of sample contracts. Of these provisions, half state that no reductions are allowed for time lost because of any illness or disability, and 40 percent state that vacations will not be reduced for absences due to occupational illness or disability. Other absences that do not result in loss of vacation under these provisions are military leave (32 percent), jury duty and union leave (each 22 percent), layoff (17 percent), funeral leave (11 percent), and other leaves or absences (13 percent).

Industry pattern: Clauses prohibiting a reduction in vacation for time lost due to specified absences are more prevalent in manufacturing (64 percent) than non-manufacturing (41 percent). They appear in a majority of contracts in 14 industries—chemicals, electrical machinery, fabricated metals, foods, furniture, leather, lumber, machinery, mining, paper, primary metals, retail, transportation, and transportation equipment.

Work During Vacation

More than half of the sample contracts studied consider the subject of work during vacations. Eleven percent of the agreements prohibit work during vacations, while 45 percent make some provision for work.

Of contracts allowing work, 99 percent impose some conditions. The employer may require work under 25 percent of these clauses, while employee consent is required under 40 percent, and union consent is required under 12 percent. Of these provisions, 9 percent specify that work will only be allowed in an emergency, and 37 percent limit work during only part of the vacation.

More than three-quarters of these clauses grant employees who work during their vacation vacation pay plus earnings, 9 percent allow employees to take a vacation on an alternate date, and 14 percent call for either method of compensation.

Industry pattern: Clauses prohibiting work during vacation appear in 9 percent of manufacturing and 15 percent of non-manufacturing agreements. Provisions allowing work during vacation are found in 56 percent of manufacturing contracts and in only 28 percent of non-manufacturing agreements. Under these clauses, employers may require work during vacation with about equal frequency in manufacturing (24 percent) and non-manufacturing (26 percent) agreements. Provisions requiring employee or union consent, however, are more common in non-manufacturing (58 percent) than in manufacturing (50 percent) contracts that permit work during vacation. Work is limited to only part of a vacation under 40 percent of the manufacturing provisions, compared to 26 percent of the non-manufacturing provisions. Employees are allowed to take a vacation on an alternate date in 12 percent of non-manufacturing provisions, compared to 8 percent of manufacturing.

Vacation Scheduling

Vacation scheduling is mentioned in 87 percent of contracts analyzed. One-half of these clauses call for plant or company shutdowns — either as a scheduled annual occurrence or an employer option. Twelve percent of these provisions allow employees to select their vacations on the basis of seniority; 65 percent call for the employer to schedule vacations, giving consideration to employee choice and seniority; and 15 percent simply state that the employer will consider individual employee preferences. Vacation scheduling is considered a management prerogative under 4 percent of the vacation scheduling provisions.

Industry pattern: Plantwide vacation shutdowns are far more prevelant in manufacturing scheduling provisions (70 percent) than in non-manufacturing (9 percent). Industries in which a majority of contracts mention the possibility of shutdowns are electrical machinery, fabricated metals, furniture, leather, lumber, machinery, mining, primary metals, rubber, stone-clay-glass, textiles, and transportation equipment.

Provisions giving management the prerogative to schedule vacations or those stipulating management will consider an employee's choice appear more frequently in manufacturing (90 percent) than in non-manufacturing (71 percent). Employee selection of vacation periods is much more common in non-manufacturing (26 percent) than in manufacturing (6 percent).

Vacation splitting is treated in 53 percent of the sample. Of these provisions, 2 percent require vacation splitting; 43 percent leave the choice to an employee; 9 percent leave the option with the employer; 40 percent call for mutual agreement.

Provisions for split vacations appear somewhat more frequently in manufacturing (55 percent) than in non-manufacturing (48 percent) agreements. The option of scheduling split vacations rests with the employer in 9 percent of non-manufacturing contracts and 8 percent of manufacturing contracts, and with the employee in 47 percent of non-manufacturing agreements compared to 41 percent of manufacturing agreements. Mutual agreement clauses appear in 43 percent of manufacturing and 36 percent of non-manufacturing industries.

Cumulation of vacations is mentioned in 50 percent of sample contracts. Cumulation from one year to the next is prohibited under 73 percent of these provisions, while 20 percent allow limited carry-over, and 7 percent allow full carry-over. Cumulation is prohibited in 80 percent of the provisions in manufacturing agreements and in 61 percent of the provisions in non-manufacturing agreements.

Vacation Rights Upon Separation _____

Vacation entitlement for employees leaving a company's service is discussed in 78 percent of contracts in the database. Of these provisions, 54 percent grant pro-rata pay for time elapsed since the most recent vacation period, 27 percent grant vacation pay only if a vacation has been fully earned, and 19 percent grant pay based on one method or the other depending on the reason for termination.

Vacation Rights Upon Separation

(Frequency Expressed as Percentage of Separation Provisions)

Vacation pay granted upon:	All Industries	Manufacturing	Non-manufacturing
Death	46	56	26
Retirement	45	56	25
Layoff	42	48	32
Quit	38	38	40
Discharge	30	29	32
Military Leave	26	33	14
Separation for any reason	17	19	14
Any separation except discharge for cause or quit without notice	10	5	19

16

Wages

Provisions calling for general wage increases were found in all but one of the 400 sample agreements in the Basic Patterns database. Cost-of-living adjustments showed a continuing decline since the 1983 study, while deferred increases showed an increase in frequency for the first time since the 1979 study.

The frequency of lump-sum payments in lieu of general wage increases and two-tier systems remained about the same as in the last survey.

Long-Term Trends In Wage Negotiations
(Frequency Expressed as Percentage of Contracts)

	1950	1954	1957	1961	1966	1971	1975	1979	1983	1986	1989	1992
Deferred increases	—	20	33	58	72	87	88	95	94	80	77	89
Cost-of-living adjustments	—	25	18	24	15	22	36	48	48	42	35	34
Wage reopeners	60	60	36	28	13	12	8	8	7	10	9	5

—Not tabulated until trend emerged.

Geographic analysis of the basic patterns database shows all contracts in the Midwest and New England provide for deferred increases, compared with 83 percent in the Southeastern region. Cost-of-living clauses and lump-sum payments appeared mainly in multiregion contracts and most wage re-openers were found in agreements in the Southeast and Southwest regions.

Provisions For Wage Adjustment
(Frequency Expressed as Percentage of Contracts in Each Region*)

	Deferred Increases	Active Cost-of-Living Escalators	Lump-Sum Payments	Reopeners
All REGIONS	89	25	23	5
Middle Atlantic	95	18	22	2
Midwest	100	21	18	4
New England	100	27	15	—
North Central	89	27	25	3
Rocky Mountain	90	20	30	10
Southeast	83	15	23	15
Southwest	85	15	15	15
West Coast	89	22	11	—
Multiregion	77	48	39	8

* See p. xi for area designations.

Other employee compensation provisions commonly mentioned in contracts include supplementary pay (shift differentials, reporting and call-back or call-in pay, temporary transfer pay, hazardous duty pay, and job-related expenses) and establishment of pay rates (incentive pay, time study, and job classification). In addition, some agreements specify hiring and individual wage progression rates.

Deferred Wage Increases ⎯⎯⎯⎯⎯⎯⎯⎯⎯⎯⎯⎯⎯⎯⎯⎯⎯⎯

Deferred increases, such as annual improvement factors and productivity increases, are called for in 89 percent of the sample—up from 77 percent in the 1989 study and 80 percent in the 1986 analysis.

Seventy-eight percent of deferred increases become effective at the beginning of the second year or, if more than one is provided, at yearly intervals. Five percent of deferred increases are paid semi-annually; 17 percent are paid quarterly or at widely varying intervals.

Industry pattern: Deferred increases are provided for in all sample contracts in the apparel, chemicals, communications, electrical machinery, furniture, leather, maritime, paper, printing, services, and utilities industries. At least 85 percent of agreements in construction, fabricated metals, foods, lumber, machinery, petroleum, primary metals, retail, and stone-clay-glass call for deferred increases.

Lump-Sum Payments ⎯⎯⎯⎯⎯⎯⎯⎯⎯⎯⎯⎯⎯⎯⎯⎯⎯⎯⎯⎯

Lump-sum payments, other than Christmas and year-end bonuses, are found in 23 percent of contracts in the database—29 percent in manufacturing and 13 percent in non-manufacturing. Eighteen percent of the database provides for first-year payments, including ratification bonuses; 15 percent defer lump sums to later years.

Industry pattern: Lump-sum payments are found most frequently in transportation equipment (56 percent). Industries with a 33 percent to 50 percent frequency of such payments are electrical machinery, fabricated metals, leather, lumber, rubber, and stone-clay-glass. No lump sums were found in apparel, construction, paper, and utilities sample contracts.

Cost-Of-Living Provisions ⎯⎯⎯⎯⎯⎯⎯⎯⎯⎯⎯⎯⎯⎯⎯⎯

The frequency of cost-of-living provisions has declined from a peak of 48 percent of contracts in the 1983 and the 1979 Basic Patterns surveys to 34 percent in the 1992 analysis. COLAs are more common in manufacturing (42 percent) than in non-manufacturing (20 percent) agreements.

Of the 135 agreements with these provisions, 35 froze adjustments over the contract term. Active c-o-l clauses appear in 33 percent of manufacturing contracts and in 12 percent of non-manufacturing. Because details of frozen c-o-l provisions often do not appear in contracts, analysis of formulas is based on active clauses.

All of the 100 contracts containing active provisions tie adjustments to changes in the Bureau of Labor Statistics' Consumer Price Index. Ninety-three percent of escalator provisions studied use the national All-Cities CPI as a base; 7 percent use selected city indexes.

Seventy-five percent of clauses tabulated call for adjustments of one cent for each specified percentage-point rise or change in CPI. The most frequently specified CPI movement is a 0.3 percentage point (32 percent of this type of formula), followed by 0.4 (23 percent). Adjustments based on the percentage CPI rise occur in 25 percent of active clauses.

Adjustments made at quarterly intervals appear predominately (70 percent) in manufacturing provisions; while annual adjustments are found in 12 percent. The reverse is true in the non-manufacturing sector where 79 percent of clauses call for annual COLAs and 16 percent for quarterly adjustments.

A limitation is placed on the amount of a c-o-l increase in 23 percent of the clauses analyzed. On an annual basis the most common ceiling or cap found in provisions with limits is 15 cents per hour (22 percent) followed by 10 cents and 20 cents (each 13 percent). The remainder range from maximum annual increases of 3 cents to 50 cents.

Under 34 percent of the c-o-l clauses, increases are paid only if CPI rises to a predetermined level. Any increase then granted is tied to the rise beyond such specified point.

Minimum adjustments, regardless of the rise in CPI, are guaranteed in 6 percent of active c-o-l clauses. Some contracts "float" accumulating COLAs above the base rate to prevent any affect on benefits tied to wages. Part or all of a float is folded or rolled into base rates at least once during contract term under 44 percent of active c-o-l clauses. Roll-ins generally occur at the beginning of a contract or annually.

Wage reductions in the event of a CPI decline are prohibited in 11 percent of c-o-l provisions included in the study. A variation limiting the reduction—usually to the level of base wages at the beginning of the contract—is found in 23 percent of these clauses.

Industry pattern: Active c-o-l clauses are found in at least one-half of contracts in transportation equipment (71 percent), apparel (67 percent), and rubber (50 percent). Freezes occurred most frequently in furniture (33 percent), followed by fabricated metals (21 percent), and primary metals and transportation (each 20 percent). No construction, leather, lumber, paper, petroleum, textiles, or utilities industry sample contracts contain COLA provisions.

Wage Reopeners

Reopeners for the renegotiation of wages during the contract term are found in 5 percent of the sample. Such clauses are found in 5 percent of manufacturing agreements and in 5 percent of non-manufacturing agreements.

Wage Structures

Two-tier wage systems set rates of new hires below those of employees already on the payroll. Tabulated in this section are lower rates that continue beyond the first six months of service. Twenty-seven percent of contracts in the database contain two-tier wage plans. Under 60 percent of these provisions, rates for new hires eventually catch up with those of more senior workers. Thirty-seven percent of the two-tier systems permanently lower pay for new hires. Three percent lay out a mixed system such as permanent two-tier rates for lower grades and temporary two-tier rates for higher grades.

Industry pattern: More than one-half of sample contracts in the retail industry (56 percent) provide for two-tier wages, followed by: foods (48 percent), transportation (44 percent), fabricated metals (42 percent), and transportation equipment (41 percent). None of these provisions were found in communications, construction, lumber, mining, petroleum, and textiles.

Hiring rates set lower than standard rates for up to six months are specified in 11 percent of sample contracts—16 percent in manufacturing and 4 percent in non-manufacturing. Such provisions stipulate that newly hired employees automatically advance to the regular job rate after a specified period of time.

While under these clauses hiring rates range from 10 cents to $7.00 below standard hourly rates, 15-cent and $1.00 differentials are the most common (each 18 percent), followed by 50 cents, 60 cents, and $1.20 (each 12 percent).

Time periods required to reach the standard rate vary from 30 days to six months. The most common period specified in these clauses is 180 days (24 percent), followed by 60 days (22 percent), 90 days (11 percent), and 30 days (8 percent).

Wage progression systems specifying rate ranges rather than single rates appear in 49 percent of contracts—48 percent in manufacturing and 50 percent in non-manufacturing. Progression from minimum to higher rates in a range may be based on length of service (73 percent of such systems), or may be affected by merit (27 percent).

Periodic review of employees' progress to determine eligibility for progression to the next step in the range is required in 12 percent of wage progression systems.

Supplementary Pay

Extra pay for late shifts is required in 86 percent of contracts surveyed—93 percent in manufacturing and 74 percent in non-manufacturing. The absence of shift premiums in most of the remaining contracts simply reflects a lack of late-shift work.

Shift-differentials are flat cents per hour payments in 73 percent of contracts with one night shift, 72 percent of second-shift premiums and 68 percent of third-shift premiums. In the remainder of these clauses, premiums are a percentage of the base rate, vary from job to job, or offer the same pay for fewer hours.

Higher premiums are paid for third shifts than for second shifts in 86 percent of contracts that schedule second and third shifts; the same premiums are paid for both second and third shifts in 12 percent.

Median cents-per-hour premiums are 31.25 cents for contracts with one night shift, 27.75 cents for second shifts, and 35.5 cents for third shifts. Median percentage premiums are 7 percent (of the base rate) for second shifts and 10 percent each for third shifts and night shifts.

Second-Shift Differentials

	Cents Per Hour[1]						Percentage of Hourly Pay[2]					
	1-10¢	11-20¢	21-30¢	31-40¢	41-50¢	Over 50¢	Up to 3%	Over 3-6%	Over 6-9%	Over 9-12%	Over 12-15%	Over 15%
All Industries	7	31	30	11	11	9	9	39	7	34	2	9
Manufacturing	6	37	30	13	10	5	10	40	3	40	—	7
Non-manufacturing	11	15	30	4	17	23	7	36	14	21	7	14

[1]Frequency expressed as percentage of contracts calling for cents-per-hour second-shift differentials.
[2]Frequency expressed as percentage of contracts calling for second-shift differentials based on a percentage of hourly pay.

Third-Shift Differentials

	Cents Per Hour[1]						Percentage of Hourly Pay[2]					
	20¢ and under	21-30¢	31-40¢	41-50¢	51-60¢	Over 60¢	Up to 3%	Over 3-6%	Over 6-9%	Over 9-12%	Over 12-15%	Over 15%
All Industries	18	25	22	12	11	11	3	8	16	47	16	11
Manufacturing	21	28	25	9	9	9	—	8	17	58	8	8
Non-manufacturing	11	15	15	22	20	17	7	7	14	29	29	14

[1]Frequency expressed as percentage of contracts calling for cents-per-hour third-shift differentials.
[2]Frequency expressed as percentage of contracts calling for third-shift differentials based on a percentage of hourly pay.

Night-Shift Differentials

	Cents Per Hour[1]						Percentage of Hourly Pay[2]					
	1-10¢	11-20¢	21-30¢	31-40¢	41-50¢	Over 50¢	Up to 3%	Over 3-6%	Over 6-9%	Over 9-12%	Over 12-15%	Over 15%
All Industries	21	23	21	8	10	15	—	13	—	75	6	6
Manufacturing	29	29	18	—	11	11	—	9	—	91	—	—
Non-manufacturing	13	17	25	17	8	21	—	20	—	40	20	20

[1]Frequency expressed as percentage of contracts calling for cents-per-hour night-shift differentials.
[2]Frequency expressed as percentage of contracts calling for night-shift differentials based on a percentage of hourly pay.

Industry pattern: All sample contracts in the following industries provide for shift differentials: chemicals, communications, electrical machinery, fabricated metals, lumber, machinery, mining, paper, rubber, transportation equipment, and utilities. At least 85 percent of agreements in construction, foods, petroleum, primary metals, stone-clay-glass, and textiles include these provisions.

Reporting pay for employees who report for work as scheduled but find no work available is guaranteed in 80 percent of the contracts. The prevalence of reporting-pay provisions is much greater in manufacturing (93 percent) than in non-manufacturing (60 percent).

The guarantee is inapplicable under 68 percent of the reporting-pay provisions if work is unavailable for reasons beyond the company's control, and under 32 percent if an employee refuses other available work.

The amount of reporting pay guaranteed varies from one to eight hours. Of contracts containing reporting-pay guarantees, 64 percent guarantee four hours of pay; 14 percent, two hours; and 13 percent, eight hours. Under 10 percent of these provisions the guarantee is increased if an employee actually begins work.

Reporting Pay

(Frequency Expressed as Percentage of Reporting Pay Provisions)

	Guaranteed Hours							
	Up to 1%	Over 1% -2%	Over 2% -3%	Over 3% -4%	Over 4% -5%	Over 5% -6%	Over 6% -7%	Over 7% -8%
All Industries	1	14	4	64	1	1	—	13
Manufacturing	—	6	4	77	—	1	—	8
Non-manufacturing	4	34	2	30	1	1	—	26

Industry pattern: Reporting pay appears in all contracts in the fabricated metals, furniture, leather, lumber, machinery, mining, paper, primary metals, rubber, and textiles industries, and in at least 85 percent of agreements in chemicals, construction, electrical machinery, foods, petroleum, stone-clay-glass, and transportation equipment.

Call-back or call-in pay, to cover situations in which employees are called in or back to work at some time other than their regularly scheduled hours, is guaranteed in 68 percent of the sample—77 percent in manufacturing and 53 percent in non-manufacturing.

Amount of call-back or call-in pay guaranteed varies from two hours to eight hours. Guarantees most frequently are four hours (63 percent of the provisions), followed by two hours (19 percent), and three hours (11 percent). In only 4 percent of these provisions are the guarantees increased if an employee actually begins work.

Premium rates are guaranteed in 34 percent of call-back or call-in clauses, with 12 percent paying premiums only for hours actually worked.

Under 9 percent of call-back or call-in clauses employees may quit work as soon as the required work is accomplished, even though the full guarantee-time has not been worked and other work is available. Six percent of the provisions specify that other work may be assigned until guarantee time has elapsed, and 13 percent invalidate the guarantee if work is prevented due to causes beyond control by the company.

Call-Back, Call-In Pay

(Frequency Expressed as Percentage of Call-Back, Call-In Provisions)

	Guaranteed Hours							
	Up to 1%	Over 1% -2%	Over 2% -3%	Over 3% -4%	Over 4% -5%	Over 5% -6%	Over 6% -7%	Over 7% -8%
All Industries	—	19	11	64	1	1	—	3
Manufactur-ing	—	14	9	72	1	1	—	3
Non-manu-facturing	—	29	18	46	—	3	—	5

Industry pattern: All sample contracts in the chemicals, mining, petroleum, and utilities industries contain call-in or call-back guarantees, while 85 percent or more of those in the communications, electrical machinery, machinery, paper, printing, and transportation equipment industries call for guarantees.

Pay for temporary transfer is provided in 65 percent of sample agreements—75 percent in manufacturing and 50 percent in non-manufacturing. Transfer to a higher-rated job is covered in 62 percent of contracts; transfer to a lower-rated job in 53 percent.

Transfer to a higher-rated job clauses most frequently (66 percent) state that the higher rate will be paid immediately. Thirty-one percent of these grant the higher rate but exclude temporary transfers of short duration, and 4 percent specify that the old rate be retained.

Of contracts providing for transfer to a lower-rated job, 95 percent specify retention of the old rate. Immediate rate cuts are stipulated in 3 percent of these provisions; cuts after a time lag are called for in 2 percent.

Hazardous work premiums are provided for in 13 percent of the sample. These premiums are found in the following industries—chemicals, communications, construction, foods, machinery, maritime, mining, paper, petroleum, retail, rubber, services, textiles, transportation, transportation equipment, and utilities. Premiums for "dirty work" appear in 5 percent of contracts studied and are found in eight industries—chemicals, construction, machinery, maritime, paper, transportation, transportation equipment, and utilities.

Travel expenses necessitated by the job are considered in 32 percent of contracts in the database—57 percent in non-manufacturing and 16 percent in manufacturing. Many agreements contain several types of expense-reimbursement provisions, falling in the categories listed below:

(1) Expenses when away from headquarters—48 percent of travel expense provisions—found primarily in communications, construction, maritime, petroleum, transportation, transportation equipment, and utilities.

(2) Mileage rate for use of own car when on company business—41 percent of such provisions—appearing mainly in communications, construction, maritime, retail, services, and utilities.

(3) Daily allowances for travel—36 percent of travel expense provisions—concentrated in communications, construction, maritime, transportation, and utilities.

(4) Moving and transfer expenses—36 percent of expense provisions—found most frequently in communications, primary metals, transportation, transportation equipment, and utilities.

Travel Expenses

(Frequency Expressed as Percentage of Contracts*)

	Car Mileage	Expenses Away from Home Office	Flat Daily Travel Allowance	Moving and Transfer
All Industries	13	15	11	11
Manufacturing	3	7	4	8
Non-manufacturing	28	28	23	16

*Many contracts contain more than one type.

Work clothes required by the job, not including safety clothes and equipment (see Section 95), are considered in 34 percent of contracts surveyed. Such provisions appear in 21 percent of manufacturing contracts and in 56 percent of non-manufacturing agreements. Work clothes provisions most often appear in transportation (76 percent); chemicals (75 percent); retail, services, and utilities (each 70 percent); foods (62 percent); construction (45 percent); and communications (40 percent).

Employers are required to supply work clothes in 69 percent of contracts that discuss the subject. This requirement prevails in retail (70 percent), services (67 percent), transportation (64 percent), and chemicals (56 percent).

The cost of laundering or replacing work clothes is borne by employers in 48 percent of these provisions.

Tools required on the job are discussed in 27 percent of contracts (20 percent in manufacturing and 37 percent in non-manufacturing). Employers supply the tools in 62 percent of such provisions and furnish replacements in 48 percent.

Bonuses, other than direct production bonuses, are provided in 7 percent of agreements studied. While there is little concentration on any particular type of bonus, Christmas and year-end bonuses are typical.

Establishment of Wage Rates

Incentive or piecework pay is discussed in 31 percent of contracts analyzed. Five percent of the agreements either prohibit establishment of an incentive plan or require union consent to adopt a plan. Incentive provisions appear in 45 percent of manufacturing agreements and in only 9 percent of non-manufacturing contracts. Implementation of incentives is barred or restricted in 6 percent of manufacturing agreements and in 4 percent of non-manufacturing contracts.

Most agreements that mention incentive operations do not elaborate on details of the system. Typical provisions primarily concern the union's role in setting or protesting standards, safeguards against speedups or rate cutting, and rules for conducting time studies.

Of contracts discussing establishment of new incentive rates or production standards during the contract term (24 percent of the sample), 70 percent permit the company to establish new rates without union participation, 20 percent call for consultation with the union, and 11 percent require union consent.

Limitations on rate revision are imposed in 72 percent of contracts containing systems incentives. Sixty-six percent of limiting clauses state that rates shall be changed only when an element (such as method, material, equipment, or product) of the job changes. 33 percent specify that the change be substantial. Thirty-four percent of limiting provisions allow revision when an existing rate is in error; many permit changes for more than one reason.

Industry pattern: Incentive provisions are found in 89 percent of sample contracts in apparel. Other industries in which at least one-half of the agreements mention incentives are electrical machinery, fabricated metals, furniture, leather, machinery, mining, primary metals, rubber, stone-clay-glass, and textiles. Such clauses are nonexistent in the petroleum and printing industries, and are rare in the non-manufacturing sector (if sales commission arrangements are not considered).

Time-study plans are found in 33 percent of manufacturing contracts and in only one non-manufacturing (retail industry) contract.

Contracts may include one or more of the following typical conditions contained in time-study provisions:

(1) Observation by a union representative allowed during a time study (3 percent).

(2) Special training provided for union time-study representatives (17 percent).

(3) Availability of time-study records to employees or union required (24 percent).

(4) Availability of records required only in case of dispute (17 percent).

(5) Timing limited to an "average" or "normal" employee (56 percent).

(6) Notice to employee and/or union when a job is being timed (36 percent).

(7) Requirement that fatigue and personal allowances be built into rate (44 percent).

Special procedures for handling time-study disputes (other than the grievance procedure) are included in 64 percent of time-study clauses. Joint reexamination by union and management is called for in 56 percent of the procedures; by the company alone, in 17 percent. Unions are permitted to check the study under 19 percent of the procedures. Eight percent of these clauses require that time-study disputes be heard by an arbiter specially qualified to deal with such disagreements (usually a trained industrial engineer).

Disputes are subject to grievance procedures and/or arbitration in 53 percent of time-study clauses.

Industry pattern: At least one-half of the contracts in the following industries contain time-study procedures: furniture, leather, rubber, and textiles. A third or more of fabricated metals, electrical machinery, machinery, primary metals, stone-clay-glass, and transportation equipment agreements include these procedures. Such clauses are nonexistent in apparel, lumber, petroleum, and printing, and in all non-manufacturing industry agreements except the one in retail.

Job classification procedures for changing or establishing new categories during the contract term are spelled out in 60 percent of the sample—71 percent in manufacturing and 41 percent in non-manufacturing.

Of agreements containing job classification procedures, 43 percent require union consultation or notification before a classification may be changed or established; 36 percent require the company to negotiate with the union. Job classification is considered a management prerogative under 9 percent of classification procedures and is subject to review by a joint labor-management committee under 8 percent.

Disputes are subject to grievance procedures in 53 percent of the provisions. Arbitration is called for under 42 percent of the clauses.

Industry pattern: Job classification clauses are found in at least three-quarters of agreements in eight industries: paper (93 percent), electrical machinery (90 percent), lumber (86 percent), mining (83 percent), transportation equipment (82 percent), machinery (81 percent), and chemicals and leather (each 75 percent).

Wage Provisions By Industry
(Frequency Expressed as Percentage of Industry Contracts)

	Deferred Increase	Active Cost-of-Living	Lump Sums	Wage Reopening	Two-Tier System	Wage Progression	Reporting Pay	Call-Back, Call-in	Temporary Transfer	Wage Incentive	Job Classification	Shift Differential	Hazard/Dirty Pay	Travel Expenses	Work Clothes	Tools
ALL INDUSTRIES	89	25	23	5	27	49	80	68	65	31	60	86	13	32	34	27
MANUFACTURING	89	33	29	5	27	48	93	77	75	45	71	93	7	16	21	20
Apparel	100	67	—	—	11	33	78	11	56	89	11	22	—	—	—	33
Chemicals	100	13	19	—	38	63	88	100	88	19	75	100	13	6	75	31
Electrical Machinery	100	35	45	—	35	85	90	90	70	60	90	100	—	15	10	15
Fabricated Metals	84	47	42	—	42	42	100	79	79	53	68	100	—	16	5	5
Foods	90	19	19	5	48	48	86	76	86	14	62	90	10	19	62	38
Furniture	100	17	17	—	17	17	100	67	83	67	67	67	—	—	17	17
Leather	100	—	50	—	25	100	100	25	75	50	75	75	—	—	—	25
Lumber	86	—	43	—	—	14	100	71	71	14	86	100	—	—	29	14
Machinery	88	46	27	4	19	85	100	88	88	58	81	100	8	8	23	4
Paper	100	—	—	—	29	21	100	86	100	7	93	100	7	—	14	21
Petroleum	86	—	14	—	14	14	86	100	86	—	71	86	14	29	29	43
Primary Metals	92	32	24	—	24	28	100	56	72	68	72	96	—	24	12	12
Printing	100	13	13	38	13	25	50	88	63	—	38	75	—	13	13	25
Rubber	50	50	33	33	17	—	100	67	83	83	50	100	17	—	33	17
Stone-Clay-Glass	92	31	38	—	8	23	85	69	62	69	69	92	—	—	8	31
Textiles	50	—	10	50	—	40	100	50	80	70	50	90	10	—	20	10
Transportation Equipment	79	71	56	—	41	65	97	94	50	35	82	100	24	47	3	24
NON-MANUFACTURING	90	12	13	5	25	50	60	53	50	9	41	74	23	57	56	37
Communications	100	20	20	—	—	100	30	90	90	—	70	100	10	100	40	30
Construction	90	—	—	14	—	3	93	21	24	—	17	97	48	69	45	72
Insurance & Finance	71	14	29	—	14	86	—	14	43	14	43	57	—	—	—	—
Maritime	100	38	13	—	38	25	25	38	25	—	13	25	75	75	38	13
Mining	75	8	17	8	—	8	100	100	100	50	83	100	33	25	17	67
Retail	85	19	19	4	56	63	56	33	33	11	48	67	4	44	70	33
Services	100	7	15	4	26	44	56	59	52	7	48	59	7	37	70	4
Transportation	84	20	16	—	44	80	64	64	48	4	24	60	20	72	76	48
Utilities	100	—	—	10	20	90	30	100	100	10	50	100	50	90	70	30

Working Conditions: Safety and Health; Discrimination

Provisions expressing an individual employee's interest in broad areas beyond the contractual protection of wages, jobs, and benefits are included in most union agreements. Occupational safety and health and non-discrimination, for example, were each dealt with in at least 88 percent of agreements comprising the Basic Patterns database.

Occupational Safety and Health

Occupational safety and health clauses are found in 88 percent of the 400 sample agreements. Geographic analysis shows that such provisions are included in from 70 percent to 100 percent of contracts in areas designated in the database.

Safety-health clauses vary considerably. Some contracts merely contain a general statement of responsibility for the safety and health of employees, while others go into detail and consider such issues as safety equipment, first aid, physical examinations, investigation of accidents, employee obligations, hazardous work, safety committees, and substance abuse.

Industry pattern: Safety and health clauses are included in 96 percent of manufacturing agreements and 76 percent of non-manufacturing contracts. These provisions appear in all rubber, mining, leather, primary metals, fabricated metals, chemicals, petroleum, textiles, printing, and maritime contracts. At least 80 percent of agreements in all other industries except utilities and communications (each 70 percent), services (67 percent), retail (63 percent), and insurance and finance (29 percent) contain safety and health provisions.

Of contracts with safety and health clauses, 40 percent include a statement that the company will comply with federal, state, and/or local laws, and 68 percent include a general statement of responsibility for employees' safety and health. Fifty-three percent of the general statements apply to both management and union; the remainder apply only to the employer.

Safety equipment, such as guards and shields around machinery and safety boots and goggles to be worn by employees, is mentioned in 43 percent of the sample contracts. Of these provisions, 60 percent specify that the company will furnish all safety equipment at no cost to employees, and 11 percent state that employees will share some of the cost (often for replacements only) of wearing apparel.

First aid supplies and/or facilities are provided for in 22 percent of the contracts studied—26 percent in manufacturing and 17 percent in non-manufacturing. A requirement that a registered nurse be on duty, at least during the day shift, is found in 19 percent of first aid clauses. A stipulation that at least one employee or supervisor trained in first aid be present at all times is included in 20 percent of these provisions.

Physical examinations are required in 32 percent of the sample. Of these clauses, 26 percent require physicals of new hires, 34 percent require physicals when employees are rehired or return to work from layoff or leave, and 58 percent require physicals periodically or at management's request. Employees may appeal an unfavorable opinion under 42 percent of the physical examination provisions.

Safety and Health Provisions

(Frequency Expressed as Percentage of Industry Contracts)

	Provisions	General Statement of Responsibility	Company to Comply with Laws	Safety Equipment	Company Provides First Aid	Physical Examinations	Accident Investigations	Hazardous Work Provisions	Safety Committees
ALL INDUSTRIES	88	60	35	43	22	32	20	28	50
MANUFACTURING	96	68	35	49	26	33	26	29	65
Apparel	89	22	67	—	—	—	22	11	67
Chemicals	100	69	13	63	38	50	25	44	69
Electrical Machinery	90	60	45	40	20	15	10	10	30
Fabricated Metals	100	84	53	84	32	32	26	37	79
Foods	95	52	29	38	24	48	10	19	62
Furniture	83	67	33	33	—	—	17	33	50
Leather	100	50	25	25	—	25	—	—	50
Lumber	86	43	14	29	14	—	—	—	57
Machinery	92	81	23	54	15	31	23	19	69
Paper	93	50	14	21	36	21	7	7	43
Petroleum	100	29	—	—	14	100	86	29	86
Primary Metals	100	80	52	68	60	48	56	64	88
Printing	100	50	50	—	—	—	—	—	—
Rubber	100	100	83	100	50	67	67	33	100
Stone-Clay-Glass	92	38	31	46	15	31	15	23	54
Textiles	100	100	30	40	10	—	—	20	40
Transportation Equipment	97	88	32	68	29	44	44	47	85
NON-MANUFACTURING	76	46	35	32	17	30	10	26	27
Communications	70	40	—	20	10	—	—	20	50
Construction	90	41	76	52	10	3	10	34	7
Insurance & Finance	29	14	14	—	—	—	—	—	—
Maritime	100	75	63	75	50	75	—	63	38
Mining	100	92	58	100	50	83	67	67	100
Retail	63	37	19	—	22	33	—	15	4
Services	67	44	30	11	7	19	4	7	22
Transportation	80	36	24	32	16	60	4	28	32
Utilities	70	70	10	40	—	—	30	20	50

Investigation of on-the-job accidents are discussed in 20 percent of the sample contracts—26 percent in manufacturing and 10 percent in non-manufacturing. Just over one-half (51 percent) of these provisions call for joint company-union investigation of accidents; 43 percent call for company investigations and require that the union be given reports; 6 percent call for company investigations and require that the union have access to the records.

Employee obligations in maintaining safety and health standards are stated in 38 percent of agreements included in the study. These provisions are found in 42 percent of manufacturing contracts and 31 percent of non-manufacturing contracts.

The most common requirement appearing in employee obligation provisions is obedience of all safety rules (69 percent). Other employee obligation clauses require that workers use safety equipment (40 percent), report all injuries (29 percent), and report any unsafe working conditions (16 percent). Disciplinary action is specified for violation of safety rules under 44 percent of contracts in which employee obligations are discussed.

Industry pattern: Employee obligations are specified in at least one-half of agreements in rubber (83 percent), paper (79 percent), mining (58 percent), chemicals (56 percent), stone-clay-glass (54 percent), construction (52 percent), and leather and textiles (each 50 percent). These provisions appear in at least one-quarter of contracts in all other industries with the exception of apparel, printing, services, petroleum, communications, utilities, retail, and insurance and finance.

Employee Obligations

(Frequency Expressed as Percentage of Employee Obligation Provisions)

	All Industries	Manu-facturing	Non-manufacturing
Must Obey Safety Rules	69	68	71
Must Report All Injuries	29	29	27
Must Use Safety Equipment	40	49	23
Must Report Unsafe Working Conditions	16	17	15
Disciplinary Action for Violation of Rules	44	42	48

Joint company-union pledges to encourage employees with substance abuse problems to seek rehabilitation are found in 43 (up from 36 in the 1989 study and 27 in the 1986 study) of the 400 sample contracts. The frequency of these provisions in manufacturing agreements remained the same as in the 1989 study, 28; the frequency in non-manufacturing agreements almost doubled from 8 in 1989 to 15 in this study. The number of contracts permitting or mandating substance abuse testing, tracked for the first time in the 1989 analysis and found in 11 agreements, jumped to 52 in this analysis.

Hazardous Work

Clauses placing some type of restriction on employee performance of hazardous work are found in 28 percent of agreements contained in the database—29 percent in manufacturing and 26 percent in non-manufacturing. Of these clauses, 56 percent state that employees are not required to engage in work they believe is unsafe, 36 percent stipulate that employees may file a grievance if required to work under abnormally hazardous conditions, and 26 percent guarantee employees the right to refuse hazardous work. Only four of the 400 contracts grant rate retention rights during temporary transfers because of hazardous conditions or injuries. The number of agreements containing "Right To Know" clauses which require employers to identify the presence of harmful or toxic substances more than quadrupled from only seven in the 1989 study to 32 in this analysis.

Safety and Health Committees

Joint management-union safety and health committees are called for in one-half of sample agreements, and are found in more than twice as many (65 percent) manufacturing agreements than in non-manufacturing contracts (27 percent). Periodic committee meetings are specified in 71 percent of contracts providing for such committees; periodic inspections of the plant in 46 percent. Pay for time spent on committee activities during regular work hours is stipulated in 41 percent of safety-health committee clauses. Issues left unresolved may be referred to a grievance and/or arbitration procedure under 29 percent of these provisions. Nineteen percent of committee provisions state that the union's role in health-safety issues is strictly advisory and not subject to liability for any illness or injury.

Safety and Health Committees

(Frequency Expressed as Percentage of Committee Provisions)

	All Industries	Manu-facturing	Non-manufacturing
Periodic Meetings	71	73	62
Periodic Inspections	46	48	41
Pay for Time Spent on Committee Activities	41	41	38
Disputed Issues Subject to Grievance & Arbitration	29	26	38

Inspections and Investigations

Inspections and investigations by government occupational safety and health officers are discussed in 12 percent of agreements analyzed. All of these provisions state that a union representative may accompany a safety-health inspector touring the premises; 50 percent specify pay for time spent in government investigations and inspections.

Industry pattern: Inspection and investigation by health and safety officers is mentioned in 58 percent of mining and 50 percent of rubber contracts and in at least 25 percent of fabricated metals, transportation equipment, leather, and chemicals contracts.

Safety and Health Provisions

(Frequency Expressed as Percentage of Contracts in Each Region*)

	Middle Atlantic	Midwest	New England	North Central	Rocky Mountain	Southeast	Southwest	West Coast	Multiregion
Provisions	85	79	89	91	70	92	100	80	94
General Statement of Responsibility	52	43	65	69	60	72	62	49	56
Company to Comply with Laws	37	29	35	28	50	26	23	51	44
Safety Equipment	35	21	35	45	50	43	62	38	62
Company Provides First Aid	16	11	23	26	–	26	8	16	42
Physical Examinations	26	25	12	35	10	26	62	27	56
Accident Investigation	16	11	8	21	20	13	31	20	40
Hazardous Work Provisions	18	18	12	23	40	30	31	24	62
Safety Committees	45	39	50	54	30	51	69	38	65

* See p. xi for area designations.

Guarantees Against Discrimination ⸻

Guarantees against discrimination—by either the union, the company, or both—appear in 96 percent of the sample. Geographic analysis reveals that non-discrimination provisions are found in from 80 percent to 100 percent of contracts in designated areas contained in the database.

Thirty-five percent of contracts containing non-discrimination clauses include a statement that any federal, state, and/or local laws prohibiting discrimination will be complied with.

Discrimination on the basis of race, color, creed, sex, national origin, or age is banned in 87 percent of agreements analyzed. Fifty-one percent of these clauses extend the ban to one or more of the following conditions: political activity or affiliation; marital status; mental or physical handicap; Vietnam veteran status; sexual preference.

A majority of anti-discrimination provisions (94 percent) either apply the ban to both management and union or make no reference to either party. Only 6 percent of these clauses apply to management alone.

Industry pattern: Ninety-one percent of manufacturing agreements and 80 percent of non-manufacturing contracts contain provisions prohibiting discrimination on the basis of race, color, creed, sex, national origin, or age. Such clauses are found in from 80 percent to 100 percent of all sample contracts except those in transportation (64 percent), insurance and finance (71 percent), construction (72 percent), maritime (75 percent), and apparel (78 percent).

Discrimination because of union membership or non-membership is prohibited in 60 percent of the sample. The ban applies only to management in 46 percent of these provisions and only to the union in 6 percent. The remainder either apply the ban to both union and management or make no reference to either party.

Industry pattern: Discrimination because of union membership is prohibited in 59 percent of manufacturing agreements and 62 percent of non-manufacturing contracts. Such provisions are found in all contracts in petroleum, 89 percent in fabricated metals, 75 percent in mining, 74 percent in services, 71 percent in insurance and finance, and in at least one-third of contracts in all other industries except apparel, and rubber.

Discrimination because of union activity is barred in 39 percent of contracts surveyed. Of these provisions, 66 percent apply the ban only to management; the remainder either make a general statement or apply the ban to both parties.

Industry pattern: Discrimination because of union activity is prohibited in 36 percent of manufacturing agreements and in 45 percent of non-manufacturing contracts. These provisions appear in at least one-half of the agreements in insurance and finance (71 percent); retail (63 percent); communications (60 percent); fabricated metals (53 percent); services (52 percent); and leather, electrical machinery, and maritime (each 50 percent).

Equal employment opportunity pledges appear in 17 percent of contracts studied. These pledges are found in 17 percent each of manufacturing and non-manufacturing agreements. A majority (84 percent) of these provisions contain joint management-union pledges.

Non-discrimination Provisions

(Frequency Expressed as Percentage of Contracts)

	All Industries	Manu-facturing	Non-manu-facturing
Provisions No Discrimination on Basis of:	96	98	93
Race, Color, Creed, Sex, National Origin, or Age	87	91	80
Political Activity or Affiliation, Marital Status, Physical or Mental Handicap, Vietnam Veteran Status, or Sexual Preference	45	48	40
Union Membership or Non-membership	60	59	62
Union Activity	39	36	45
Equal Employment Opportunity Pledges	17	17	17